Published in 2015 by:

Helion & Company Limited
26 Willow Road
Solihull
West Midlands
B91 1UE
England
Tel. 0121 705 3393
Fax 0121 711 4075
email: info@helion.co.uk
website: www.helion.co.uk
Twitter: @helionbooks
Visit our blog http://blog.helion.co.uk

Text © Tom Cooper, Albert Grandolini & Arnaud Delalande 2014
Colour profiles © Tom Cooper 2014
Maps © Helion & Company Limited 2014
Photographs © as individually credited

Designed & typeset by Farr out Publications, Wokingham, Berkshire
Cover design by Paul Hewitt, Battlefield Design (www.battlefield-design.co.uk)

Printed by Henry Ling Ltd., Dorchester, Dorset

UK ISBN 978-1-909982-39-0
British Library Cataloguing-in-Publication Data. A catalogue record for this book is available from the British Library

All rights reserved. No part of this publication may be reproduced, stored, manipulated in any retrieval system, or transmitted in any mechanical, electronic form or by any other means, without the prior written authority of the publishers, except for short extracts in media reviews. Any person who engages in any unauthorized activity in relation to this publication shall be liable to criminal prosecution and claims for civil and criminal damages.

Cover: The appearance of R-3S-armed Su-22Ms was something of a surprise for USN fliers: This big and powerful fighter-bomber was not a very good interceptor and armed with air-to-air missiles for self-defence purposes only. (USN)

CONTENTS

MW00563873

Note: In order to simplify the use of this book, all names, locations and geographic designations are as provided in *The Times World Atlas*, or other traditionally accepted major sources of reference, as of the time of described events. Similarly, for ease of use, Arabic names are romanised and transcripted rather than transliterated. For example, the definite article al- before words starting with 'sun letters' is given as pronounced instead of simply as al- (which is the usual practice by non-Arabic speakers in most English-language literature and media).

ABBREVIATIONS

4WD	Four-wheel drive
AA	Anti-aircraft
AB	Air Base
AdA	Armée de l'Air (French Air Force)
AFB	Air Force Base (used for US Air Force bases)
AK	Russian for Automat Kalashnikova; general designation for a class of Soviet, or former East Bloc, manufactured class of 7.62mm assault rifles
ALAT	Aviation Légère de l'Armée de Terre (French Army Aviation)
AML	Automitrailleuse Légère (class of wheeled armoured cars manufactured by Panhard)
An	Antonov (the design bureau led by Oleg Antonov)
ANT	Armée Nationale du Tchad (National Chadian Armed Forces)
APC	Armoured Personnel Carrier
ATGM	Anti-tank guided missile
BAe	British Aerospace
BET	Borkou-Ennedi-Tibesti (Prefecture in northern Chad)
Brig Gen	Brigadier General (military commissioned officer rank)
CAP	Combat Air Patrol
Capt	Captain (military commissioned officer rank)
CAS	Close Air Support
CASA	Construcciones Aeronáuticas SA (Spanish aircraft manufacturer)
CBU	Cluster bomb unit
CDR	Conseil Démocratique Révolutionnaire (Democratic Revolutionary Council)
CG	Cruiser, Guided (hull designation for USN cruisers armed with guided missiles)
CIA	Central Intelligence Agency (USA)
c/n	Construction number
CO	Commanding Officer
COIN	Counterinsurgency
Cdte	Commandante (commissioned officer rank, equal to Major)
Col	Colonel (military commissioned officer rank)
Col Gen	Colonel-General (top military commissioned officer rank)
CV	Carrier, Vertical (hull designation for USN aircraft carriers)
CVN	Carrier, Vertical, Nuclear
CVW	Carrier, Vertical, Wing (composite carrier air wings embarked on board USN carriers)
DD	Destroyer (hull designation for USN destroyers)
DDG	Destroyer, Guided (hull designation for USN destroyers armed with guided missiles)
DoD	Department of Defence (USA)
EAA	Escadrille d'Appui Aérien (Air Support Squadron)
EAF	Egyptian Air Force (official title since 1972)
EC	Escadre de Chasse (Fighter Squadron)
ECM	Electronic countermeasures

ELAA	Escadrille Légère d'Appui Aérien (Light Air Support Squadron)
ELINT	Electronic intelligence
ENT	Escadrille Nationale Tchadienne (National Chadian Squadron)
ERV	Escadron de Ravitaillement en Vol (Air Refuelling Squadron)
FAN	Forces Armées du Nord (Armed Forces of the North)
FANT	Forces Armées Nationales Tchadiennes (National Army of Chad)
FNFP	Front National des Forces Progressistes (National Front of Progressive Forces)
FROLINAT	Front de Libération Nationale du Tchad (National Liberation Front of Chad)
Gen	General (military commissioned officer rank)
GMT	Groupe Mixte de Transport (Mixed Transport Group)
GUNT	Gouvernement d'Union Nationale de Transition (Transitional National Government of Chad)
HQ	Headquarters
IAP	International Airport
IFF	Identification Friend or Foe
IFR	In-flight refuelling
IFV	Infantry fighting vehicle
IR	Infra-red, electromagnetic radiation longer than deepest red light sensed as heat
Il	Ilyushin (the design bureau led by Sergey Vladimirovich Ilyushin, also known as OKB-39)
KIA	Killed in action
Km	Kilometre
LAAF	Libyan Arab Air Force
Lt	Lieutenant (military commissioned officer rank)
Lt Col	Lieutenant-Colonel (military commissioned officer rank)
1st Lt	First Lieutenant (military commissioned officer rank)
2nd Lt	Second Lieutenant (lowest military commissioned officer rank)
Maj	Major (military commissioned officer rank)
Maj Gen	Major-General (military commissioned officer rank)
MANPADS	Man-portable air defence system(s). Light surface-to-air missile system that can be carried and deployed in combat by a single soldier
MBT	Main Battle Tank
MHz	Megahertz, millions of cycles per second
Mi	Mil (Soviet/Russian helicopter designer and manufacturer)
MiG	Mikoyan i Gurevich (the design bureau led by Artyom Ivanovich Mikoyan and Mikhail Iosifovich Gurevich, also known as OKB-155 or MMZ 'Zenit')
Nav/attack	Used for navigation and to aim weapons against surface target
NCO	Non-commissioned officer

OAU	Organisation of African Unity
OCU	Operational Conversion Unit
OPEC	Organisation of the Petroleum Exporting Countries
ORBAT	Order of Battle
OTU	Operational Training Unit
PoW	Prisoner of War
RAF	Royal Air Force (of the United Kingdom)
RAM	Régiment d'Artillerie de Marine (Marine Artillery Regiment)
RCC	Revolutionary Command Council (government of Libya in the 1970s)
REC	Régiment Étranger de Cavalerie (Cavalry Regiment of the Foreign Legion)
REP	Régiment Étranger Parachutistes (Parachute Regiment of the Foreign Legion)
RIAOM	Régiment Interarmes d'Outre-Mer (Overseas Inter-arms Regiment)
RICM	Régiment d'Infanterie Chars de Marine (Marine Infantry Tank Regiment)
RIMa	Régiment d'Infanterie de Marine (Marine Infantry Regiment)
RMS	Royal Mail Ship (prefix used for seagoing vessels that carry mail under contract to the British Royal Mail)
RPG	Rocket Propelled Grenade
RWR	Radar Warning Receiver
RHC	Régiment d'Hélicoptères de Combat (Combat Helicopter Regiment)
SA-2 Guideline	ASCC codename for S-75 Dvina, Soviet SAM system
SA-6 Gainful	ASCC codename for ZRK-SD Kub/Kvadrat, Soviet SAM system
SA-7 Grail	ASCC codename for 9K32 Strela-2, Soviet MANPADS
SAM	Surface-to-air missile
SDECE	Service de Documentation Extérieure et de Contre Espionnage (Foreign Intelligence and Counterespionage Service in France)
SEPECAT	Société Européenne de Production de l'Avion d'École de Combat et d'Appui Tactique (European Company for the Production of a Combat Trainer and Tactical Support Aircraft)
SIGINT	Signals intelligence
Sqn Ldr	Squadron Leader (military commissioned officer rank, equal to Major)
Su	Sukhoi (the design bureau led by Pavel Ossipowich Sukhoi, also known as OKB-51)
SyAAF	Syrian Arab Air Force
Technical	Improvised fighting vehicle (typically an open-backed civilian 4WD modified to a gun truck)
UARAF	United Arab Republic Air Force (official title of the Egyptian Air Force, 1958–1972)
USAF	United States Air Force
USD	United States Dollar (also US$)
USN	United States Navy
USS	United States Ship
USSR	Union of Soviet Socialist Republics (or 'Soviet Union')
Wg Cdr	Wing Commander (military commissioned officer rank, equal to Lieutenant-Colonel)
WIA	Wounded in Action

CHAPTER 1
BACKGROUND

In this age when the 'Global War on Terror', 'Spread of Islamic extremism' and many related conflicts around the World, especially in Africa, dominate the headlines, few might recall the times when it was another 'war of terror' that was in the news almost every day. Even less so since the so-called 'Arab Spring', which reached its first peak with a popular uprising in Libya, in spring 2011, culminated in a lengthy intervention by forces of the North Atlantic Treaty Organization (NATO), and the collapse of the regime of Muammar Muhammad Abu Minyar al-Gaddafi, who ruled the country for no less than 42 years.[1] It is practically forgotten that the first recorded event of air warfare in history took place in the skies over Libya. This happened on 1 November 1911, when Italian military pilot Lt Giulio Gavotti flew the first 'mass-produced' military aircraft ever to attack Turkish positions.

Air power was to drop many more bombs upon Libya during the following 100 years, but quite a few bombs were to be dropped by Libyan aircraft upon other countries too. Between 1973 and 1989, various Western powers and Libya were entangled in a seemingly never-ending exchange of blows launched in retaliation for one action or the other. This confrontation resulted in a number of high-profile, even though low-scale, clashes between the Libyan Arab Air Force (LAAF), the US Navy (USN), and even the French Air Force (Armée de l'Air, AdA). The LAAF, quantitatively one of most potent air forces in North Africa and the Middle East in the 1970s and 1980, also saw intensive deployment in Chad. Initially characterised by small scale insurgency for the control of N'Djamena, the Chadian capital, this conflict eventually turned into a major war when Libya invaded the country outright. The LAAF deployed not only French-made Mirages, but also Soviet-made MiG and Sukoi fighter-bombers, Mil helicopters and even Tupolev bombers, to establish her dominance over the extensive battlefield of the Sahara Desert. Because of the Cold War, but also due to confrontation with Libya over a number of other issues, France, a one-time major arms supplier to Libya, and the USA gradually got dragged into that war. Deployments of their troops and intelligence services in Chad, Egypt and the Sudan never resulted in a full-scale war against Libya,

---

1 There are around a dozen different translations of this family name in to the English language, of which the most widespread (in the public realm) is 'Gaddafi', even though 'Qadhafi' was used more often in the official documentation of various Western countries. Interestingly, 'Gathafi' was the spelling used in his passport, when captured by Libyan revolutionaries in Tripoli on 24 Aug. 2011.

but time and again it culminated in small-scale aerial operations that proved crucial to developments on the ground, several of which are still a matter of extensive debate. Often related to issues relevant well away from Libyan borders and airspace, most of the air wars in question were never officially declared and of rather limited duration, primarily consisting of a handful of low-intensity clashes. Some were as a result of covert activities of intelligence agencies, but others resulted in full-scale battles that lasted for days, sometimes even weeks and months.

The authors grew up reading news about this conflict on an almost daily basis during the 1980s. Over the years, the 'hobby' of researching related details and the geopolitical backgrounds transpired into a profession of military aviation journalism, which resulted in this book. The story it reveals is not only the story of air wars fought over and by Libya, but also that of the pilots of many other nationalities that participated in them, and about their often rather troublesome equipment.

Our hope is that the results of our work are going to provide a unique insight into this almost forgotten conflict. An air war that raged from the skies over the southern Mediterranean to southern Chad and northern Sudan, represented a formative period of the LAAF, but which also prompted a number of crucial modifications and developments in France and the USA. Indeed, while small in scale, many of the campaigns in question served as testing grounds for modern-day doctrine, tactics and technology of air power.

Simple Geography and a Turbulent History

Libya is the fourth largest country in Africa, and seventeenth largest on the world. Clockwise, it borders Egypt in the east, Sudan, Chad, and Niger in the south, and Algeria and Tunisia in the west. Most of the terrain is characterised by extensive deserts, sand seas, extreme heat and aridity. There are no major rivers and less than 2% of the national territory receives enough rainfall for settled agriculture. The handbook entitled *Der Soldat in Libyen*, distributed to German soldiers deployed in the country with the Deutsches Africa Korps in February 1941, described the local terrain as follows:

Libya as a whole is a desert plateau, gradually dissolved by steep, rocky terrain and individual high surfaces. Scattered plump mountain massifs up to 1000 metres high are protruding over the completely flat or slightly wavy surfaces ... 50 to 100 kilometres inland the steppe zone ends and a completely dead desert begins, consisting not only of sand, but also stone and gravel.

Indeed, terrain in Libya includes only a few highlands, such as the mountain ranges near the Chadian border, the barren wasteland of the rocky Nafuza Mountains south-west of the capital city of Tripoli, and the Marj Plain with Jebel al-Akhdar ('Green Mountain') in Cyrenaica in the east. Vegetation is sparse and usually limited to date palms and olive and orange trees that grow in scattered oases, while wildlife is limited to desert rodents, gazelles, a few wildcats, eagles, hawks and vultures.

Within easy reach of Europe and with links to North Africa and the Middle East, the area has experienced quite a turbulent history over the last 3,000 years. The name of Libya is a derivative from the appellation given to a Berber tribe by the ancient Egyptians. It was very rarely used before the country's independence. Nowadays it is used by a country that came into being as an independent and unified state only in the second half of the 20th century, consisting of Tripolitania in the northwest (approximately 16% of the country's area), Cyrenaica in the east (about 51% of the country's area),

Muhammad Idris as-Senussi and his troops during their raid into Egypt in 1916. (Photo via Mark Lepko)

and Fezzan in the southwest (around 33% of the country's area). Although known to have been inhabited already some 25,000 years ago, Fezzan was only loosely governed by the Garamentes tribe from about 1,000 years BC. Greeks and Phoenicians began founding colonies on the coast of Cyrenaica and Tripolitania in the 7th and 5th centuries BC, before Carthage took over the region. The Egyptians, the Persians, the army of Alexander the Great and the Ptolemies of Egypt all ruled Cyrenaica and Tripolitania, which flourished during the Roman Empire period and even when the Vandals took over in 455. Cyrenaica and Tripolitania maintained their distinct Carthaginian and Greek cultures until their once prosperous cities were racked by political and religious unrest, and degenerated into bleak military outposts. Similarly, Fezzan developed a unique history and identity. Correspondingly, different parts of what was to become Libya have all maintained their own relations with the outside world ever since, resulting in the latent internal disunity that is characteristic of the country today.

In medieval times, Libya, or the parts thereof, continued changing hands. The Byzantinum Empire conquered the area in the 6th century, but lost it to the Arabs under Amr Ibn al-As, who conquered Cyrenaica in 643, Tripolitania in 649, and to Ukba Ibn an-Nafi, who conquered Fezzan in 663. The area was successively ruled by the Umayyads, Fatimids, and a Berber dynasty, before it was conquered by the Ottoman Empire, in the 16th century. Successive waves of Arab armies were followed by settlers that brought Islam, the Arabic language, and Arab culture to the indigenous population along the coast, but the Berbers of the interior resisted for centuries and remained linguistically and culturally separate.

Under Ottoman rule, a pasha (or 'regent') ruled the area from Tripoli, the principal city of Tripolitania, but in 1711 Ahmad Qaramanly, a Turkish-Arab cavalry officer, seized power in Tripoli and founded his own dynasty while acknowledging the Ottoman sultan as his suzerain. Following the ending of local piracy by the United States of America (USA) and European powers in the early 19th century, the economy declined and the area slipped into civil war, enabling the Ottomans to re-establish themselves in power in 1835. It was around this time that Muhammad Ibn Ali as-Senussi, a highly respected Islamic scholar from present-day Algeria, won many followers among the Cyrenaican Bedouins, and this area gradually developed into the centre of a new religious order. By the end of the 19th century, virtually all of the Bedouin in the region had pledged their allegiance to the Senussi brotherhood, and Senussis were subsequently to spearhead the nascent Libyan

To the Shores of Tripoli

Outside circles of naval historians, it is often forgotten that the history of the area nowadays within Libyan borders included a period of military conflict with the then still very young United States of America (USA). The conflicts in question, better known as the First and Second Barbary Wars, were a result of a period during which Tripolitania lapsed into military anarchy due to lack of direction from the Ottoman Empire, in the mid-18th century. The area came under the rule of successive pashas that established themselves in power through coup d'états and then continued to pay a nominal tribute to Istanbul, but otherwise ruled the area as an independent country. In order to improve the ruined economy of their states, pashas in Tripoli, Algiers, Tunis and the independent Sultanate of Morocco began to heavily employ corsairs (pirates) against European merchant shipping underway on crucial shipping routes in the Mediterranean. Alternatively, nations with an interest in protecting their shipping were forced to pay a tribute.

After the United States' independence from Great Britain was formalised by the Treaty of Paris in 1783, France ceased protecting US ships underway in the Mediterranean Sea, and a number of these were seized by corsairs. The US government reacted with diplomatic action, but this was only partially successful. While hundreds of American sailors were released from custody in Algiers and Morocco, the USA had to pay a ransom that amounted to nearly one sixth of the entire US federal budget, and was to continue paying an annual tribute to local rulers. Eventually, the US Congress passed naval legislation that, among other things,

provided for six frigates in 1801, and US President Thomas Jefferson ordered a small naval task force into the Mediterranean. There were several minor clashes in which its ships defeated some of the Tripolitanian corsairs and, in August 1801, the schooner USS *Enterprise* defeated a 14-gun polacca *Tripoli*. However, the frigate USS *Philadelphia* ran aground while patrolling Tripoli harbour in October 1803 and the crew, including Captain William Bainbridge, was captured.

In February 1804, Lieutenant Stephen Decatur led a successful raid into Tripoli, in the course of which the captured frigate was destroyed, thus at least recovering the pride of the nascent US Navy. Subsequent attacks on Tripoli were less successful and eventually the Americans organised a force of US Marines, led by 1st Lieutenant Presley O'Bannon and 500 mercenaries, that marched from Alexandria in Egypt to Derna in Cyrenaica. Concerned about this threat, the pasha in Tripoli rushed to sign a treaty with the USA and release all the Americans 'in his possession', ending this war in June 1805. Despite this success, the American practice of paying tribute to the pirate states in North Africa ended only with the conclusion of the Second Barbary War (also known as Algerine or Algerian War), fought in 1815–16.

These two conflicts and their participants were immortalised not only in the second line of the US Marine Corps' Hymn ('... to the shores of Tripoli'), but also in many of the traditional names of US Navy warships, including Bainbridge, Constellation, Decatur, Enterprise, Intrepid, Somers, and O'Bannon.

Painting 'To the Shores of Tripoli' by Raymond Massey, showing the frigate USS *Constitution* during the second attack on Tripoli on 4 August 1804.

Schooner USS *Enterprise* (right) capturing the Tripolitanian polacca *Tripoli* in August 1801. (Drawing by Capt William Bainbridge Hoff, from circa 1878; US Navy Department)

nationalist movement.

In late 1911, Italy invaded Tripolitania and Cyrenaica, forcing the Ottoman Empire to sue for peace and accept the Treaty of Laussanne the following year. Local tribesmen opposed Italian rule and initially were successful in preventing its spread beyond a few enclaves along the coast of Cyrenaica. During World War I, the Senussi first sided with the Central Powers. Encouraged by the German and Ottoman Empires, they launched the so-called Senussi Campaign, but after a disastrous raid into British-occupied Egypt in 1916, they negotiated a truce with the British and Italians, whereupon Rome accepted Muhammad Idris as-Senussi's hereditary rule in Cyrenaica. Only a few years later, the fascist leader Benito Mussolini opened the Second Italo-Senussi War. The technically superior Italian forces, led by General Badoglio, destroyed Idris' forces in Tripolitania

in 1928 and in Fezzan in 1930. Their campaign in Cyrenaica was concluded only against fierce resistance from Senussi tribesmen, in the course of which the Italians murdered over 24,000 civilians and herded around 100,000 survivors into concentration camps, forcing the others to flee into the desert. In 1934, the area was declared as 'pacified' and formally established as an Italian colony under the classical name 'Libya'. It consisted of four provinces: Tripoli, Misurata, Benghazi and Dernah and the Military District of Fezzan. Marshal of the Regia Aeronautica (RA, Royal Italian Air Force), Italo Balbo, Governor of Libya from 1934 until 1940, then called for the colonisation of Libya and started a policy of integration between the Italians and Libyans, that proved quite successful. Laws were passed that allowed Muslims to be permitted to join the National Fascist Party and created Libyan military units within the Italian

Army. The Italians invested considerably in the development of the public sector and the modernisation of agriculture, building nearly 400km of railways and more than 2,000km of roads. With the Italian population increasing to nearly 110,000, Libya was declared a part of metropolitan Italy, on 9 January 1939.[2]

Origins of Libyan Military

During the second half of the 1930s, planning to enlarge Libya to the Aouzou Strip in northern Chad (then a French colony) and establish a broad land bridge between Libya and Italian East Africa, the Italians established two divisions of Libyan colonial troops and a battalion of paratroopers. These included around 31,000 native Muslim soldiers, some of whom were granted 'special' Italian citizenship and considered 'Moslem Italians'. Initially assigned to the Royal Colonial Corps of Libya, these units participated in the Italian invasion of Ethiopia in 1936, where they were highly decorated for their distinguished performance in battle. Later on, the 1st Libyan Infantry Division was incorporated into the reserve of the 10th Italian Army, and the 2nd Libyan Infantry Division into the 13th Corps, and thus they became involved in the Italian invasion of British-occupied Egypt, launched in September 1940. In December of the same year, the British Eighth Army launched a counterattack that not only ended in the conquer of Cyrenaica, but also the destruction of the 10th Italian Army and the capture of most of their Libyan troops. During the following two years, the indigenous population of Libya became pawns in the war, with thousands being killed and most of the scarce infrastructure destroyed by the time Axis troops were forced to retreat into Tunisia in early 1943. Libya finally ended up under British Military Administration, which made use of the former Italian bureaucrats, but also began training the Libyan civil servants and police.

This also included 600 Senussi fighters who had fled to Egypt after the collapse of the resistance in 1934 whom the British organised into five battalions of the Libyan Arab Forces (LAF) which were deployed inside Libya during late 1942. They saw little fighting: instead they were primarily tasked with securing camps for German and Italian Prisoners of War (PoWs). The LAF was dissolved immediately after the war, but most of its members subsequently joined the British-established Libyan Police.

Meanwhile, British interests in Libya came into conflict with those of the French and the Soviet Union. Namely, in 1942, the Free French moved north from Chad (with British approval) and occupied Fezzan, subsequently attaching some parts of it to the French military regions of southern Algeria and southern Tunisia. Moscow, which at the Potsdam Conference in 1945 agreed that the Italian colonies seized during the war should not be returned, subsequently proposed separate provincial trusteeships and began claiming Tripolitania for itself while assigning Fezzan to France and Cyrenaica to Britain. With no end to the discussions in sight, France advocated the return of the territory to Italy, while the USA proposed a trusteeship for the whole country under the control of the United Nations (UN – whose charter had become effective in October 1945). Eventually, the conflicting interests of London and Paris left the Allies with no alternative but to refer the issue to the United Nations. Successfully representing Libya, Sidi Muhammad Idris al-Mahdi as-Senussi, the Emir of Tripolitania and Cyrenaica and the leader of the Senussi Muslim Sufi order, advocated independence for his country and on 21 November 1949, the UN

King Idris II of Libya (right), with President Gamal Abdel Nasser of Egypt in 1964. (Albert Grandolini Collection)

General Assembly approved a resolution calling for independence of a sovereign Libya by 1 January 1952. A national assembly, composed of an equal number of delegates from Cyrenaica, Fezzan and Tripolitania, convened at Tripoli in 1950 and designated Emir as-Senussi a king-designate, but also unanimously agreed that Libya would be established as a democratic and federal state, governed by a constitutional monarchy, with a cabinet and a bicameral legislature. It promulgated the Libyan constitution on 7 October 1951, and on 24 December of the same year the emir, as King Idris I, proclaimed the independence of the federal United Kingdom of Libya. Around this time, a large part of the British-established Libyan Police, especially its former LAF elements was re-organised as the Royal Libyan Army (RLA).[3]

The Senussi King's Air Force

Traditionally, Libya was an agricultural country, but due to lack of water, farming and raising livestock remained restricted to the coastal regions, as it does even today. Following independence, with the infrastructure in tatters, 90% of the population being illiterate and the sale of scrap metal salvaged from battlefields of World War II representing the largest source of revenue, this nascent nation was heavily dependent upon financial aid from Great Britain and the USA. Although King Idris banned the work of all political parties and practically abolished the federal state in 1952, the following year London and Washington began providing development aid in exchange for rights to maintain military installations in the country. The British and Libyan governments signed a 20-year treaty of friendship and alliance, granting the Royal Air Force (RAF) the use of base at el-Adem, south of Tobruk, and the rights for the 25th Armoured Brigade of the British Army to remain based in the country. Furthermore, King Idris' government and the USA signed an agreement that granted the US Air Force (USAF) the use of Wheelus Air Force Base (AFB) outside Tripoli, including a depot

2   Vittoria Capresi, *I centri rurali libici di fondazione – architettura e urbanistica (1934–1940)*, Institut für Kunstgeschichte, Bauforschung und Denkmalpflege, Wien, 2010.

3   Philip S Jowett, *The Italian Army, 1940–45: Europe 1940–1943* (Oxford, Osprey, ISBN 978-1-85532-864-8); Kenneth Ciro Paoletti, *A Military History of Italy* (Greenwood, ISBN 0-275-98505-9); Piero Crociani, *Le Uniformi Coloniali Libiche, 1912–42*; Edmund Hall, *The Italian Army in Egypt During World War II* (egyptstudycircle.org.uk); James Burd, *Libyan and National Paratrooper Units, 1940–41* (Comandosupremo.com, Feb. 2010).

Libya's first military pilot, al-Hadi Salem al-Husomi, who graduated from training in Turkey in 1957. (al-Husomi Collection)

President Nasser donated two Helwan-built Gomhouria trainers to the RLAF in 1962. (David Nicolle Collection)

Only seven out of sixteen F-5A/Bs, including this example, were delivered to Libya in 1969. (Albert Grandolini Collection)

One of two F-5Bs given to Libya in 1969 at Wheelus AB, with Libyan and USAF pilots preparing to embark for a training flight. (Tom Cooper Collection)

The sole C-47B donated to the RLAF by USAF in the 1960s. Notable are the fin flash and roundel in red, black and green. (Albert Grandolini Collection)

for the storage of nuclear weapons and several practice firing ranges, subject to renewal in 1970.

During the 1950s, Libya therefore experienced a period of very slow economic growth largely depending on the provision of foreign aid. The situation changed dramatically in June 1959, when the Esso Corporation (later renamed Exxon) discovered huge reserves of high-quality oil and gas, especially after the exploitation and export of these began in 1962. This effected a profound change in the economy, with gross domestic product increasing nearly tenfold by the end of that decade. However, the oil boom created social and economic problems that the royal government was neither able nor willing to address. Although financing a number of major public works projects, expanding educational and health services, and supporting low-cost housing, small businesses and industries, King Idris was first and foremost a Cyrenaican, with a Cyrenaican's political and economic interests and power base. He was never at ease with Tripolitanians, nor with a military including

them, especially because many of the RLA officers were openly sympathetic to the ideas of President Gamal Abdel Nasser of Egypt, calling for Libya to become involved in the Arab struggle against Israel. The net result was massive mistrust of King Idris by his own military, which was kept very limited in size. Totalling only 6,500 men, the RLA was countered by two rival paramilitary units, the National Security Force and the Cyrenaican Defence Force. Nearly all of the units of these three branches were commanded by loyal,

Members of the RCC, which established itself in power in Tripoli and Benghazi, on 1 September 1969. Gaddafi is standing in the centre. (Gaddafi Collection)

September 1969: a youthful Capt al-Gaddafi addresses a crowd in Tripoli, shortly after taking over as the de facto head of state. (Gaddafi Collection)

The Libyan population supported the September 1969 Coup and participating military units were cheered by civilians, as can be seen on this photo from the streets of Tripoli. (Albert Grandolini Collection)

for fear of a possible coup attempt. Learning about al-Husomi's problems, the Egyptians stepped in and donated two Helwan Gomhouria basic trainers (based on the design of a Bücker Bü.181, manufactured under licence in Egypt), but the Americans and the British swiftly intervened in order to interrupt relations with Cairo. Instead, Washington intensified its involvement and donated two Lockheed T-33A jet trainers, two Bell 47B helicopters, the first of several Douglas C-47B transports and began training about 20 Libyan pilots and ground personnel at Wheelus AFB.

During the following years, the build-up of the RLAF continued at a slow pace. When King Idris negotiated the withdrawal of British and US troops from their bases in Libya in 1966, the USAF instructors working in the country suggested the government lease 16 Northrop F-5A and two F-5B Freedom Fighter jet fighters. A corresponding contract was signed the following year and a group of 20 RLAF pilots and 37 technicians were sent for training in the USA. They returned to Wheelus in 1969, together with the first seven F-5As, and a USAF team that supervised the aircraft's introduction into service with the RLAF.

Despite this important development, and the excellent training it received, the air force remained a very small branch of only 400 officers, NCOs and other ranks, and its future did not appear especially bright. Indeed, even after the introduction of the F-5, fully qualified pilots remained so scarce that many had to fly different aircraft types as required (even the commander of the RLAF, al-Husomi, regularly had to fly T-33As and C-47s). The situation was similar in other branches of the military.[4]

1969 Coup d'État

King Idris' suspicion of his military was no paranoia. Nasser's popularity and the spread of Arab nationalism within the RLA, coupled with resentment over corrupt royals and the families they favoured, prompted several officer cliques to start plotting a take-over. After the king announced his intention to abdicate in favour of the Crown Prince Sayed Hassan ar-Rida al-Mahdi al-Senussi, effective on 2 September 1969, he travelled to Turkey to rest. A group of about 70 young officers from the Signal Corps, mostly captains in their late twenties, organised as the Free Officer's Movement, set their plan in motion.[5] Surprising almost everyone,

but often poorly qualified Cyrenaicans, and equipped with only the bare minimum of necessary armament.

Only after considerable pressure from Washington, which offered aid for the further development of Libya's armed forces, did the Defence Minister, Abd al-Nabi Yunis, issue a decree according to which the first RLA pilot, al-Hadi Salem al-Husomi, quite fresh from training in Turkey, was to establish the Royal Libyan Air Force (RLAF) on 13 September 1962.

Al-Husomi therefore found himself facing a number of almost insurmountable problems. With good roads existing only along the coast, connecting Tripoli with Tunisia and Egypt, through Benghazi and Tobruk, air transport always played an important role. Indeed, more than a dozen minor airfields were constructed by the Italians, Germans and the Allies before and during the WWII. Many more were built during the 1960s, when they served companies involved in oil and gas exploitation. However, King Idris refused to provide the necessary financing for either aircraft or personnel for the RLAF,

---

4 Dupuy et al., pp. 223–225; Flintham, pp. 93–94; Stanik, pp. 12–20; Cooper et al., *Arab MiGs Vol. 4*, pp. 193–202.

5 Dissent within the RLA was so widespread, that at least one other group of officers was planning its own coup attempt to take place a few days later. Their plan was overtaken by subsequent developments.

they outmanoeuvred their superiors and the loyal monarchists with a well-executed plot that brought all police bases, radio stations, government offices and airports in Tripoli and Benghazi (the then twin capitals of Libya) under their control within just 24 hours, and the rest of the country soon after on 1 September 1969. The bloodless coup was enthusiastically supported all over the country, and even by members of royal establishment. Hassan ar-Rida was arrested, together with all other senior civil and military officials of the royal government, but a few days later he publicly renounced all rights to the throne and stated his support for the new government. He was released into exile in Egypt, where King Idris eventually settled too.

Meanwhile, the Free Officers Movement proclaimed an end to the monarchy and the foundation of the Libyan Arab Republic, governed by command councils in Tripoli and Benghazi, which in turn exercised power by giving orders to soldiers and civilians via radio. Real power, however, was concentrated in the hands of the Revolutionary Command Council (RCC). The RCC abolished parliamentary institutions, continued the prohibition of all political parties, and assumed all legislative functions, announcing Libya's neutrality in the Cold War, opposition to all forms of colonialism and imperialism, but also its dedication to Arab unity and to the support of the Palestinian cause against Israel. During the following weeks, the RCC split into two groups; one consisting mostly of civilians, supporting the Minister of Defence, Lt Col Adnan al-Hawaz; the other centred around Captain (later self-promoted in rank to colonel) al-Gaddafi and consisting of pragmatic idealists who were inclined toward demagoguery flavoured with Arab-Islamic motifs. The latter group eventually won the power struggle, and fastened its grip on power. Gaddafi was recognised as leader of the RCC and the commander-in-chief of the armed forces, becoming the de facto head of state. At that time, few could imagine what far-reaching consequences this development would have for the future not only of Libya and its air army, but also Egypt, the Arab–Israeli wars, and many other conflicts in Africa and even Europe.

CHAPTER 2
MILLION-MAN ARMY

With the coup completed, the RCC proceeded with its intention of consolidating itself in power and modernising the country. The new administration introduced widespread economic and social reforms, significantly boosting the prosperity of the entire nation through funding compulsory education for all, providing medical care at no cost and a number of similar measures. The Council proclaimed the trade terms for Libyan oil and gas as unfair and began exercising pressure upon foreign companies, forcing them to increase prices, a tactic soon followed by the Organisation of the Petroleum Exporting Countries (OPEC) with far reaching consequences. During the following years, the RCC pursued a policy of increasing state control over the petroleum sector until it was all nationalised in September 1973, in turn securing immense revenues for Libya. Furthermore, the new administration sought to undermine the power and prestige of various tribes (assailing them as impediments to unity and social progress), while bringing the legal code into compliance with Sharia Laws.

Instant Air Force
Planning a significant expansion of the armed forces of the newly-created Libyan Arab Republic, as well as military cooperation with Egypt and other Arab states, primarily those involved in continuous struggle with Israel, the RCC assigned Lieutenant Colonel (Lt Col)

By September 1969, the LAAF operated several C-47s, and this example was one of the first to receive the new national markings in pan-Arabic colours, as well as the new official title: Libyan Arab Republic Air Force. (Albert Grandolini Collection)

Mahdi Saleh al-Farijani as the new commander of the Libyan Arab Air Force (LAAF). Formerly a pilot of King Idris' personal Lockheed JetStar, Farijani's first order was to search for an alternative source of vital quantities of arms and equipment.[6]

In the days following the coup, the new Libyan administration invited representatives of Great Britain, France, USA and the Union of Soviet Socialist Republics (USSR or Soviet Union) for negotiations. Hoping to secure their military bases and economic interests, but also because the RCC avoided any commitments, they quickly extended diplomatic recognition of the new administration. Indeed, in 1970 Washington even informed Gaddafi about at least one planned counter-coup. However, British and US attempts to

The first LAAF commander, Lt Col Mahdi Saleh al-Farijani, once flew this Lockheed JetStar that primarily served as VIP transport for King Idriss. (Albert Grandolini Collection)

6 Although the official title of Libya was changed several times during the 42 years of Gaddafi's reign, and the air force was to adapt its official title accordingly, 'LAAF' remained in colloquial and official use until 2011. It is therefore used everywhere in this book, and instead of titles like 'LARAF' (for 'Libyan Arab Republic Air Force') or 'LAJAF' (for 'Libyan Arab Jamahiriya Air Force'), although the latter two were sometimes used for official purposes, and even applied on several transport aircraft.

USAF personnel seen at Wheelus AFB during the ceremony of closure of the installation on 30 June 1970. (Albert Grandolini Collection)

The 53 Mirage 5Ds ('D' stood for 'Décembre', French for December – the month in which the corresponding contract was signed) ordered by Libya in 1969 were very similar to the Mirage 5J version originally developed for Israel. This example was photographed in France prior to delivery. (Fana de l'Aviation Archive)

form a working relationship failed. Concluding that cooperation with Western powers might not be tolerated by the Libyan peple, and always severely critical of the West for its support of Israel, in December 1969 Gaddafi agreed with London a withdrawal of all British forces from Libya by 30 March 1971, and with Washington for all US installations to be vacated by 30 June of the same year. Concluding that Wheelus AFB had lost its strategic importance, the administration of US President Richard M. Nixon did not mind this loss, but in return it cancelled the delivery of the remaining eight F-5As. Nevertheless, it did accept a Libyan order for sixteen Lockheed C-130H Hercules transports and granted permission for delivery of eight of these.[7]

Cooperation with the USSR initially proved impossible, primarily for ideological reasons. The RCC was categorically rejecting communism and instead concluded that cooperation with France was the most promising, largely because the French were popular in the Arab world of the late 1960s and because of their imposition of an arms embargo on Israel. Furthermore, Libya had already developed close ties with Paris, centred around a major oil deal, and Farijani was keen to obtain the supposed 'winning weapon' of the June 1967 Arab–Israeli War, the Dassault Mirage fighter-bomber. Unsurprisingly, negotiations proceeded swiftly, and in December 1969 the Libyan Ministry of Defence placed an order for 53 Mirage 5D fighter-bombers, 32 Mirage 5DE interceptors, ten Mirage 5DR reconnaissance fighters, 15 Mirage 5DD two-seat conversion trainers, 12 Magister jet trainers, ten SE.316B Alouette

IIIs and nine Aérospatiale SA.321M Super Frelon helicopters.[8]

Even with hindsight, it is hard to gauge whether Gaddafi and Farijani were aware of the fact that the small LAAF would require years just to recruit and train enough personnel to maintain and fly all these aircraft, not to mention the ability to develop the infrastructure necessary to operate them. Pending the release of relevant official documentation, it is impossible to conclude whether they ordered such huge numbers of aircraft for specific, well-founded reasons, or out of sheer enthusiasm and naivety. Abdoul Hassan, who served with the LAAF at that time, explained:

Gaddafi embarked on a massive plan to equip a one million man Muslim armed force. He ordered massive acquisitions of all kinds of weapons. This part of his plan was not difficult to implement. But the part related to recruiting and training the necessary manpower was. We did not even have enough adequately trained commanders to prepare and then realise that plan. Our commanders did not have the experience to properly develop and manage such a force. And then, of course, other political factors put the brakes on this uphill drive.[9]

Certainly enough, shortly after ordering Mirages the LAAF began recruiting large numbers of young Libyans for training as future pilots and ground personnel, as recalled by Hazem al-Bajigni:

I joined the LAAF in 1971 and was sent to Yugoslavia with about 35 other pilot cadets and over 90 future engineers and technicians. Our class was the second to go to Vazduhoplovna Vojna Akademia in Mostar [the air force academy of the former Air Force and Air Defence Force of Yugoslavia, since 1992 part of Bosnia Hercegovina]. Of course, all Libyans were treated with scepticism by Yugoslav officers as they thought of us as 'some illiterates from Africa'. But already our senior class proved them wrong. We proved ourselves as good or better than the average Yugoslav cadet.

---

7   The rest of that order was subsequently cancelled too, possibly in reaction to Gaddafi's demands for Malta not to permit NATO to use any of its airfields – in exchange for provision of Libyan financial aid, in 1971.

8   As regards the designations of Libyan Mirage variants, 5D stood for 'Décembre' (French for December); 5DE stood for 'Décembre Electronique'; 5DR for 'Décembre Reconnaissance'; and 5DD for 'Décembre Dual', see Hervé Beaumont, *Mirage III, Mirage 5, Mirage 50: Toutes les versions en France et dans le Monde* (Clichy Cedex, Guides Larivière Vol. 19, 2005, ISBN 2-848980-079-2).

9   Abdoul Hassan (name changed due to concerns about his and his family's security), interview, May 2003; this and all subsequent quotations from Abdoul Hassan are based on transcription of the same interview.

One of ten SE.316B Alouette III helicopters purchased for the LAAF from France in 1971. They were primarily used for search and rescue purposes. (Albert Grandolini Collection)

Cooperation with Egypt

Deeply pious and ascetic, influenced by Nasser's fiery speeches on the Voice of the Arabs radio station in Cairo, Arab defeats in Palestine in 1948 and during the June 1967 Arab–Israeli War, Gaddafi entered an especially close cooperation with the Egyptian President and eagerly invited Egyptians to help plan the expansion of the Libyan military. Keen to obtain training bases outside the reach of the Israeli Defence Force/Air Force, and also to get their hands on the French-made Mirages, the Egyptians were quick to grab the opportunity. Indeed, before long, Farijani offered to loan some of their Mirages to the United Arab Republic Air Force (UARAF, as the Egyptian Air Force was officially named between 1958 and 1972), and so in fact, ten out of the twenty Libyan pilots that travelled to France for the first Mirage conversion course in early 1970, were actually Egyptians, including Captain Mohammad Fathi Fat-hallah Rif'at:

I did my conversion course at Dijon. We were a mix of pilots from MiG-17, MiG-21, and Su-7 units that underwent that course. This was good because the Mirage was a multi-role jet. We then returned to Libya to fly Mirage 5Ds for training; which were ground-attack jets. There was a big difference between the Su-7 and the Mirage. The Su-7 had a good engine, reasonable payload, but poor manoeuvrability. The Mirage had good manoeuvrability, better acceleration, good visibility out of the cockpit and much better avionics. Foremost, the Mirage had a much better range. It could take two times as many bombs as the Su-7 over double the range.[10]

Instead of questioning how a small air force such as the LAAF could suddenly find such a significant number of experienced fighter pilots, and at the same time be involved in the clandestine delivery of Mirage 5 fighter-bombers to Israel (despite an arms embargo officially imposed upon Israel in 1967 and 1969), the French followed what had become an informal policy of 'don't ask, don't tell' in regards of arms sales to the Middle East. One of the

The first Mirage officially delivered to Libya was this 5DD two-seat conversion trainer. Not camouflaged, but already wearing Libyan national markings, it participated in a military parade in Tripoli in September 1970. (Albert Grandolini Collection)

Unlike the Mirage 5DE, the Mirage 5D that was delivered to Libya was not armed with air-to-air missiles, but offered a very potent fighter-bomber capability, which the Egyptians were determined to fully exploit. (Albert Grandolini Collection)

Egyptian pilots trained in France, Mohammed Okasha, recalled:

The French were a little bit surprised that our French interpreter was speaking Russian too. At the time there were no Russians in Libya, so this was very unusual. But they did not ask any

---

10 Rif'at, interview, Oct. 2002; this and all subsequent quotations from Rif'at are based on transcription of the same interview.

Gaddafi was strongly influenced by the pan-Arabic ideas of his idol, Gamal Abdel Nasser and the two leaders quickly tied a close friendship. (Gaddafi Collection)

Since the Mirages were still not operational, and with the French threat to cancel further deliveries to Libya if any of the aircraft were donated to Egypt, when Gaddafi visited Cairo to sign the Treaty envisaging a new United Arab Republic, his aircraft was escorted by LAAF F-5As. (via Tom Cooper)

One of the Libyan Mirage 5Ds seen shortly after its arrival at Birma/el-Tanta in Egypt. The aircraft already wears the revised fin flash, introduced during attempts to establish a new union between Egypt, Libya and Syria in spring 1972. (Albert Grandolini Collection)

questions … our relations were very good, and there was lots of mutual understanding and rapprochement.

Furthermore, considering the extensive facilities Libya inherited from the British and Americans, which the LAAF could hardly use, the UARAF was granted permission to deploy its Operational Training Unit (OTU) to the former RAF el-Adem, renamed as Gamal Abdel Nasser Air Base (GANAB). The OTU in question was soon expanded to an operational unit, Air Brigade 306, the work of which, as was usual for the entire UARAF at that time, was supervised by a Soviet air warfare instructor, Viktor Nikolayevich Lopatchenko. During his stay in Libya, Arabic-speaking Lopatchenko used the pseudonym Captain Abdul Kasim as-Shaybani. Although not remaining in the country for very long, it was in this fashion that Soviet military advisers appeared in Libya for the first time. Another Soviet instructor, Colonel Victor K Babich, who acted as Senior Advisor for Air Combat Tactics to the Syrian Arab Air Force (SyAAF) during the October 1973 War with Israel, explained about the importance of Lopatchenko's presence in Libya as follows:

When we arrived in Syria, in the spring of 1973, we concluded that Syrian pilots had no tactics. They flew by intuition. We tried to organise them. We first underwent a detailed study of the enemy. This is where Libyan Mirages were so valuable, because they

offered us firsthand experience with the look and manoeuvring capabilities of the Israelis. After flight-testing Mirages, we developed a training program for Syrians, starting with such manoeuvres like break, reverse, slip, and the more complex ones, like high-yo-yo, barrel roll and others. That way they we trained Syrians in the 'fundamentals' of air combat.[11]

Attempted Union

Very early during his reign, Gaddafi began promoting the need for a single Arab state stretching from Casablanca to Baghdad, and entered related negotiations with several Arab statesmen. Already in December 1969 he had founded the Arab Revolutionary Front with Egypt and Sudan, and invited Syria to join. Convinced that a combination of Libyan petroleum wealth and Egyptian military strength would result in a dominant power in the Arab world and beyond that would invigorate the struggle against Israel, he reinforced promotion of a union between Egypt and Libya following Nasser's death in September 1970, and entered corresponding negotiations with the new Egyptian President, Anwar as-Sadat. Always cautious, Sadat instead suggested the creation of a political federation that

11 Col Viktor Babich, 'Egyptian Interceptors in War of Attrition', *Istoriya Aviaciy* Magazine (in Russian), Vol. 3/2001.

President Sadat, Libyan strongman Gaddafi and President Assad sign the agreement that envisaged the creation of a 'new' United Arab Republic including Egypt, Libya and Syria in September 1971. For a number of reasons, this plan was never realised. (via Group 73)

would lead to a slow unification. An unofficial charter of merger was signed by the two leaders in February 1972, but never implemented as Sadat became increasingly wary of Gaddafi's ever more radical ideas and unpredictability.[12]

Despite differences between Gaddafi and Sadat, military cooperation between Egypt and Libya was continued during the build-up of Arab militarisation prior to the October 1973 War with Israel. The first Mirages were delivered to Libya in early 1971, and officially entered service with No. 1001 Squadron LAAF, which acted as the Operational Conversion Unit (OCU) and was supervised by several Pakistani instructors. Subsequent batches of Mirages were assigned to the newly-established No. 69 Independent Squadron UARAF, which was working under the command of Colonel (Col) Ali Zien al-Abideen Abdul-Jawwad, with Mohammed Okasha as Deputy. Unaware that around the same time France was clandestinely delivering Mirage 5s to Israel as well, Okasha recalled:

It was with quite some pride that we received Mirages built and equipped to precisely the same standard as originally planned for delivery to Israel. However, we did not use them as interceptors. The Mirage 5DEs were armed only with one Matra R.530 air-to-air missile, but these proved troublesome to operate. Instead, our main armament consisted of two 30mm cannon and up to eight French-made 250kg (551lb) bombs or 32 unguided rockets. The primary reason was that we were in such an urgent need

of more potent, long-range fighter-bombers, and the Mirage 5 offered us an unprecedented capability in terms of range at low altitude, bomb-carrying capability, and precision of delivery. The Mirage was vastly superior to the MiG-17 and Su-7. Sure, the MiG-17 was cheap, and easy to maintain and fly, but the Mirage could carry twice as many bombs as the Su-7 and four times as many as the MiG-17.[13]

While very little is known about the work-up process of No. 1001 Squadron LAAF, numerous accounts about the subsequent development of No. 69 Squadron UARAF became available in recent years. The Egyptians rotated several of their MiG-21-units to GANAB, in order to offer their pilots an opportunity for dissimilar air combat manoeuvring exercises. Okasha continued:

After working up our unit, in 1972 we were also involved in exercises with our MiG-21 pilots, with the purpose of teaching them about the capabilities of our new aircraft and helping them develop tactics for countering Israeli Mirages.

Amongst the UARAF MiG-21-pilots sent to Libya was Medhat Zaki:

---

12 Blundy et al., p. 75.

13 Okasha, interview, Nov. 2011 & Okasha, *Soldiers in the Sky*, Chapter 3, p. 2; unless otherwise stated, this and all subsequent quotations from Okasha are based on transcriptions of the same interview.

Egyptians and early Libyan Mirage pilots were supervised by several Pakistani instructors, headed by Sqn Ldr Farooq Umar, contracted for this purpose in 1971 and stationed at Ukba Ibn Nafi AB. This 1973 photograph shows (from left to right): unknown, Flg Off Atikhan (background), Flt Lt Imtiaz Hayder (later an air marshal) and Flt Flt Lt Najeeb Akhtar (a specialised photo-reconnaissance pilot and later an air marshal). Hayder and Akhtar both served as Mirage instructor pilots in Libya. (Farooq Umar Collection)

In 1972 we travelled to Libya to train against the Mirages, and to benefit from the expertise of our own and Pakistani pilots. We were briefed on Mirage 5s and only then realised how much more advanced that type was in comparison to the MiG-21. Their fuel reserves were amazing. We flew lots of mock combats against the Pakistanis.[14]

Despite all the possible agreements and signatures, the plan for a new United Arab Republic was never realised. Nevertheless, this attempt left its mark upon the national insignia applied to aircraft operated by the Egyptian and Libyan air forces. While both of the services used the pan-Arabic colours of red, white and black, the Egyptians added the 'Eagle of Sallahaddin' in the spring of 1972, when the UARAF returned to its Egyptian Air Force (EAF) identity. With a few exceptions, the crest was not applied on LAAF aircraft. The mirages were handed over to No. 69 Squadron once the 25th aircraft arrived at the former Wheelus AFB, re-named as Umm Aittitiqah (colloquially known as Mitiga) in early 1972. Fully equipped and combat ready, the UARAF unit returned to Egypt about a year later, as recalled by Okasha:

After some ten months of training during which each pilot flew around 100 hours on the type, our squadron moved to Tanta AB, on 7th April 1973. We arrived there followed by several transports carrying spares and ammunition, as well as our technicians. As soon as we settled at Tanta, we started flying again, but our operations were somewhat hampered by limited amounts of ammunition and spares the Libyans provided to us. As of that time, the squadron was still under the command of Col al-Jawad, with seventeen pilots qualified to fly ground attacks and two pilots trained to fly the reconnaissance variant. We were all very experienced and nobody had less than 1,500 hours in his log book. These twenty pilots had nineteen Mirage 5Ds and two Mirage 5Rs at their disposal. The Libyan Mirage squadron

was still working up and they were to follow us to Egypt only in November 1973.

Behind them, the Egyptians left the second group of their pilots that was undergoing conversion training on Mirages in Libya. One of them is known to have been involved in a crash of a LAAF Mirage 5DD on 15 May 1973. He ejected together with his Pakistani instructor, Tahir Alam, but suffered multiple fractures on both legs.[15]

An unpredictable Partner

Some of several nails in the coffin of the proposed union were delivered by a combination of Israeli, Libyan and US actions. On 21 February 1973 a Libyan Arab Airlines Boeing 727 (registration 5A-DAH), on Flight 114 from Tripoli via Benghazi to Cairo, missed its destination due to a navigational error and entered the airspace over Israeli-occupied Sinai, heading straight for former UARAF Bir Gifgafa Air Base, occupied by the Israelis during the June 1967 War and renamed Refidim. After the crew realised their mistake, they corrected their course but the airliner was intercepted soon after by two McDonnell Douglas F-4E Phantom IIs. Initially, the 727's crew failed to understand the hand signals of the Israeli pilots, who called on them to follow. Only seconds after the Libyan pilot and his French co-pilot finally realised that the fighters they could see outside their cockpit belonged to Israel, the Phantoms opened fire. Using their General Electric M61 Vulcan 20mm cannons, they hit both wings, then the cabin, and then knocked out two engines, causing the Boeing to burst into flames. Around 12.11, two minutes after the attack, the Libyan passenger aircraft exploded low above the ground while trying to make a forced landing in the desert of western Sinai, killing 100 of the 104 crew members and passengers.

While the Israeli government subsequently entangled itself in multiple contradictions in attempting to explain why its fighters had opened fire upon and shot down an obviously unarmed civilian airliner (and after some Israelis had ridiculed the 727 crew's attempt to make an emergency landing in western Sinai as 'botched up'), Gaddafi was infuriated by Egypt's failure to prevent this tragedy. In retaliation, he ordered Farijani to prevent the use of airspace off the Libyan coast to US aircraft. On 13 March 1973, five LAAF Mirage 5s intercepted a Lockheed C-130B-II of the 7406th Contracted Support Squadron USAF off the coast of Tripoli and fired several warning shots in front of it. On 11 October 1973, in reaction to the US provision of military aid to Israel during the war with Egypt and Syria, the Libyan administration notified the US State Department that the Gulf of Syrte was to be closed and considered a part of Libya's territorial waters. A line along the 32° 30' Parallel, roughly connecting Misurata and Benghazi, was declared 'The Line of Death', and Gaddafi threatened to shoot down any foreign aircraft that would cross it in southerly direction.[16] Furthermore, Gaddafi planned to sink RMS *Queen Elizabeth II*, a British liner chartered by American Jews to sail to Haifa for Israel's 25th anniversary in May 1973. His attempts to persuade the crew of an Egyptian submarine, temporarily put under Libyan command as part of the two nations' drive towards unity, to launch this attack were discovered by the government in Cairo and overruled and the sub was ordered straight back to Alexandria.[17]

14 Zaki, interview with Group73, Nov. 2011.

15 Mike Bennett, *Chronological Listing of Libyan Air Force Losses & Ejections* (ejection-history.org.uk).

16 Mark, C. R., *Congressional Research Service Issue Brief for Congress: Libya*, Foreign Press Centers, US Department of State, 10 Apr. 2002.

17 Ian Birrell, 'The Pariah who tried to Sink the QE2 – then fooled Blair and the West', *Daily Mail*, 21 Oct. 2011.

The wreckage of Libyan Arab Airlines Boeing 727 5A-DAH, shot down by two Israeli Phantoms on 21 February 1973, killing 100 of the 104 crew members and passengers. (IDF)

President Sadat finally distanced himself once and for all from the Libyan leader. While their militaries continued to cooperate, their personal relations became openly hostile and only worsened during and after the October 1973 War. Namely, although Gaddafi considered himself a close Egyptian ally, and although Libya financed several military-related projects in Egypt, Sadat did not inform Libyans about his and Syrian intentions to launch a war for the liberation of the Sinai Peninsula and the Golan Heights on 6 October 1973. Gaddafi considered this a crucial issue as Libya was already involved in supporting several Palestinian militias: the Popular Front for the Liberation of Palestine (PFLP), the Abu Nidal Organisation and the Black September group that perpetrated the 1972 Munich massacre of Israeli athletes in West Germany. He was granting them rights to establish training camps inside Libya and he felt personally offended; mid-way through that conflict he ordered the LAAF to return all of the Mirages handed over to Egypt. Okasha recalled the following incident with two Libyan officers dispatched by Farijani to forward corresponding demands:

Just two days into the war, on 8th October, two LAAF officers arrived at Tanta to negotiate the return of the Mirages. We asked them to be reasonable and explained to them that combat operations were in full swing. It would be madness to withdraw the Mirages. They continued insisting and this discussion became very fierce, ending in a fist-fight between them and one of our pilots.

Although both officers returned to Libya empty handed, the LAAF eventually decided to also deploy No. 1001 Squadron to Egypt, two weeks later. However, this unit did not participate in the war against Israel for reasons summarised by another experienced Egyptian pilot and historian, Gabr Ali Gabr:

Generally, we could not make much use of other Arab pilots

because their standards of training and qualifications were, by and large, and in some cases considerably, lower than those of our pilots. Therefore, during the October 1973 War with Israel, they were deployed only in rear areas, far from the front line and only under special circumstances. For example, Libyans lacked experience and caused a number of landing accidents on their arrival in Egypt, resulting in damage to several Mirages. Their standards were extremely low. Of our other allies, the Algerians were better than the Libyans, but still not as good as our pilots.[18]

Furthermore, no sooner than No. 1001 Squadron reached Egypt, Gaddafi was enraged by Sadat's offer of a cease-fire with Israel, as explained by Okasha:

Two days after the cease-fire of 24th October, Libyans deployed several large transport aircraft loaded with commandos and technical personnel to Tanta, with orders to secure and dismantle the Mirages and bring them back to Libya, if necessary by force. Our air defences prevented them from even approaching our air base. Immediately after the cease-fire, a big disagreement erupted at the highest levels of political leadership between Egypt and Libya. Libyans complained bitterly about the results of the war: they considered them much too limited, and thus expressed fierce criticism about President Sadat's decision to accept a cease-fire. Gaddafi complained about Syria, as well as the Jordanian decision not to enter the war. He described the war as nothing more than an attempt to modify the status quo with Israel, and thus a cowardly act. From his standpoint, no other result was acceptable other than the destruction of Israel.

Although being in possession of more than a clear picture about the actual situation, Gaddafi subsequently presented a completely

18 Gabr Ali Gabr, interview, Apr. 2005; this and all subsequent quotations from Gabr are based on transcriptions of the same interview.

Scene from the Libyan Air Force Academy in Misurata, as seen during a visit by the Hungarian Air Force delegation in the 1970s. At that time, this was one of the most modern institutions of its kind around the world. (Robert Szombati Collection)

Libya was the largest export customer for SOKO G-2 Galeb and J-21 Jastreb training jets of Yugoslav origin, which served as jet trainers at the academy in Misurata. This photograph is showing the G-2 serial number 10201 in markings introduced following the short war with Egypt in July 1977. (Photo by Chris Lofting)

wrong image to the public, exaggerating the achievements of LAAF Mirage pilots in the war against Israel. On 19 May 1974, the Libyan newspaper al-Fatah reported, 'the Libyan Arab Air Force made some 400 sorties against the Israelis'. Contradicting even his own statements, Gaddafi further went as far as to claim to Western and Arab reporters that Libya, 'had not sold, loaned or given any weapons to the Egyptian Government', while immediately afterwards he would proudly add to the same audience that it was LAAF pilots that were helping train the Egyptians 'how to fly'. Because no Egyptian attempts to challenge such statements became known outside the Arab world, most Western publications continued repeating his claims for the next 30 years. Thus the actual small number of combat sorties flown by Mirages of No. 69 Squadron EAF during the October 1973 War, remains unknown amongst the general public.[19]

The dispute over Mirages continued into July 1974, when President Sadat wrote a letter to the RCC confirming the use of Libyan aircraft, but also protesting, 'recent unfriendly Libyan actions against Egypt and the Egyptian government, including demands for the return of the Mirages still in Egypt'. Sadat indicated that his letter was a response to another Libyan request for the return of Mirages on the grounds that, 'the combat role of the aircraft in association with the October War was now terminated, and that the aircraft were urgently needed in Libya'. Several days later, a similar Libyan request was addressed to Egyptian War Minister Ahmed Ismail, and to EAF commander Maj Gen Hosni Mubarak by Col Abu Bark Younes, Chief-of-Staff of the Libyan Army. After both Egyptian generals replied that this was not a military matter but should be decided by the political leaders, Sadat eventually ordered the return of Mirages.[20]

Actually, by that time the situation had reached the point at which Sadat considered launching a war against Libya. It is known that he requested that the US National Security Adviser, Henry Kissinger, exercise pressure upon the Israeli government not to launch an attack on Egypt in case his forces were involved in a war with Libya.[21]

19 The story in question is outside the scope of this book, and is therefore going to be provided in detail in the book *Arab MiGs Vol. 5*.

20 AW&ST, July 1974; ironically, until news about this exchange of letters became known in the West, the French stubbornly maintained that no Libyan Mirages were ever transferred to Egypt.

21 Memorandum of Conversation (between Henry Kissinger and Golda Meir), 01043, 1 Mar. 1974, released in response to FOIA inquiry.

Expansion at any Price

The October 1973 Arab–Israeli War resulted in several important experiences for Gaddafi. He realised that no amount of diplomatic or economic pressure, not even an oil embargo, could force Washington to stop supporting Israel. One of the major problems Egypt and Syria experienced during the October War was the issue of resupplying their depleted stocks of arms and ammunition, which made them heavily dependent on Soviet readiness to provide these. Gaddafi concluded that countries with poorly developed or non-existent defence industries were often disowned by the superpowers. This led to his decision to turn Libya into the 'Arsenal of Islam', with a huge weapons cache; the country was not only to become capable of fighting Israel independently from other Arab states and superpowers, but also to become influential through obtaining the capability to provide armament to other allies at his own discretion.

Following their early experiences with France, Italy and the USA, the Libyans concluded that there was only one party capable of and ready to provide the amounts of armament and equipment deemed necessary – the Soviet Union. The positive aspect of this conclusion was that Soviet armament were as relatively easy to use even for inexperienced operators, usually available at lower prices than comparative Western armament, and within much shorter periods of time. Correspondingly, the Libyan administration subsequently established military-related commercial ties to Moscow, all the time carefully avoiding stronger Soviet political influence. In the course of negotiations that began in October 1973 and lasted well into the spring of 1974, Gaddafi demanded deliveries of hundreds of combat aircraft, over 2,000 tanks and armoured vehicles, and corresponding quantities of other equipment. An initial Soviet offer for 400 MiG-21s was turned down because by that time the LAAF was well aware about the limitations of that aircraft in comparison to Western-made fighter-bombers. Farijani insisted on the Soviets delivering a mixture of more potent types and therefore an agreement was reached according to which the LAAF was to be reinforced by 54 brand-new MiG-23MS interceptors and MiG-23UB two-seat conversion trainers, 35 MiG-23BN fighter-bombers, and 'only' 64 MiG-21bis interceptors and MiG-21UM conversion trainers by

One of the first MiG-23MS's (serial 712) as seen at Ukba Ibn Nafi AB in 1976. Notable are the launch rails for R-3S air-to-air missiles, installed on underwing pylons and under the fuselage. Another example can be seen in the background. (Tom Cooper Collection)

1976.[22] Another major contract, apparently reached in agreement with Baghdad, followed soon after, ordering fourteen Tupolev Tu-22A medium supersonic bombers, capable of reaching Israel out of bases in Libya.[23]

Furthermore, Libya entered negotiations with France for purchase of 38 Dassault Mirage F.1s, which resulted in an order officially issued on 6 January 1975, for a total of 16 Mirage F.1AD fighter-bombers (delivered between January 1978 and April 1979), 16 Mirage F.1ED interceptors (delivered between January 1978 and October 1979), and six Mirage F.1BD two-seaters (delivered between April 1978 and October 1979).[24] Finally, Italy was contracted for delivery of 20 Meridionali-Boeing CH-47C Chinook transport helicopters, deliveries of which began in 1980.

Meanwhile, used to his cadets receiving excellent training in

Yugoslavia, Farijani expected the LAAF to experience less problems while pressing for all of these new aircraft to be put into service, but especially those of Soviet origin. He envisaged the air force to accelerate training of new personnel with the help of the newly-constructed Air Force Academy outside Misurata, for which he ordered 230 SIAI-Marchetti SF.260WL Warrior trainers from Italy, and 50 SOKO G-2 Galeb and J-21 Jastreb jet trainers and light strikers from Yugoslavia. Years later, one of the former Yugoslav instructors that used to work at Misurata, recalled about the training of Libyan pilots as follows:

A group of us served as instructors in Misurata, training Libyan pilots in basic flying skills. Our pay was actually around US$5,000 a month but, as was usual practice at that time, US$3,500 were kept by the state, so we got US$1,500. Misurata was a fantastic installation, a very large air base with extensive support facilities. Amongst others they had a huge library that included every single title related to air warfare published around the world. No matter where or when, they would get a copy of the publication in question and bring it there. Additional Libyan pilots were trained in Yugoslavia. In 1974, a group of 60 was sent to the Yugoslav Air Force Academy in Zemunik AB, near Zadar [in Croatia after 1991]. Although nowadays there is still some chaff when we recollect about our Libyan students, fact is that around twenty of these 60 trainees became top pilots and officers of their air force. Military service in Libya at that time was voluntary, but some methods of recruitment were rather unusual. For example, they would organise a football match, then close all the exits and deploy military police around the stadium, with trucks waiting for recruits. Then a selection team would go inside and pick up people, 'he's going to air force, him to infantry, this one is going to serve as a technician and him with the navy...!' In this fashion we got plenty of students forced to fly by political order from above, but not willing, so the drop-out rate was high. From some 150

22 Notable is that only 55 out of 64 MiG-21s purchased from the USSR actually entered service with the LAAF. The balance of nine planes were handed over to the so-called 'Force-14', which Gaddafi envisaged as the core of the future air force of an independent Palestinian State. This little known force, which included a number of Palestinians – some of whom used to serve with the SyAAF in the 1970s – was further made up of several pilots trained to fly helicopters and transport aircraft. Many of them returned to Israeli-occupied parts of Palestine (Gaza Strip and the West Bank), following the Oslo Accords in the early 1990s, where they became instrumental in indeed establishing an official flying arm that operated three Mil Mi-17 helicopters until most of these were disabled by the Israelis, in 1999.

23 Sadik, interview, Mar. 2006, in turn confirming research published in Cooper et al., 'Bombed by Blinders', *AirEnthusiast*, Vol. 116. According to Sadik, the idea was for Tu-22s to – for example – start from Libya, climb to a very high altitude and accelerate to supersonic speed, bomb Israel and then continue straight in direction of Iraq, where they could land to re-fuel and re-arm for their 'return' mission, on the way back. Together with the considerable electronic countermeasures suite carried by this type, such a modus operandi was to assure a high level of operational safety for Iraqi and Libyan Tu-22s.

24 Liébert et al., p. 220; although one F.1BD crashed on 10 Apr. 1978 (Lt Col Badiki and Lt Sagbir ejected safely), the conversion process of Libyan Mirage F.1-pilots was successfully completed and both units declared operational in late 1979.

Photographed at the same time was this early LAAF MiG-23UB two-seater conversion trainer. (Tom Cooper Collection)

One of sixteen Mirage F.1AD fighter-bombers (serial number 408) ordered by Libya, seen prior to delivery in January 1978. (Albert Grandolini Collection)

Pre-delivery photograph of the Mirage F.1ED interceptor (serial number 51), ordered by Libya in January 1976, and delivered between January 1978 and October 1979. (Photo by M Fluet -Lecerf)

cadets that joined the Military College in Mostar during the same year, only 50 qualified. Some could not learn to fly, no matter how hard we tried. In the worst case, their superiors would conclude, 'Allah shall decide'. Those that did qualify not only excelled as pilots but are kept in the highest esteem by their instructors even today. Libyan instructors always carried a stick with them, even when seated in the rear seat of a two-seater, and they would beat their students on their hands or even on the head, sometimes during the flight, if they did something wrong.[25]

Obviously, Farijani's expectations proved overoptimistic. There was no way to 'instantly' create a large air force, and even the arrival of Soviet instructors could not provide the assistance necessary to accelerate the process. Certainly, large numbers of newly-acquired aircraft were put into storage to act as a 'strategic reserve', as originally planned. However, the fact remains that no matter how much new equipment was purchased by Libya, the expansion of its military lagged well behind planning. Even as of 1976, the entire military totalled only about 30,000 officers and other ranks, eventually

25 Sinisa Klarica, 'Gadafi nije bio pitomac u Zemuniku' ('Gaddafi was no Cadet in Zemunik', in Croatian), *Zadarski List*, 24 Feb. 2011.

forcing Gaddafi to introduce compulsory military service, a measure that proved quite unpopular amongst Libyans.

Trial-and-Error Process

Except for purchasing large amounts of aircraft, Libya requested France and the USSR to help establish a ground-based, integrated air defence system covering the entire coast between Tripoli and Tobruk. Correspondingly, they began ordering French-made Crotale surface-to-air missiles (SAMs), as well as SA-2, SA-3, and SA-6 SAMs, and ZSU-23-4 self-propelled and towed ZU-23 anti-aircraft guns from Moscow. Although the French and Soviets delivered the necessary equipment, the Libyans proved unable to find enough personnel for all of it. Correspondingly, many of the foreign advisers that arrived in the country during the mid-1970s were contracted to operate the nascent air defence force, a process that was never successfully completed, instead of supervising the LAAF. Farijani was eventually forced to ask for advice and help from Syria, which resulted in an agreement with Damascus for the SyAAF to deploy 40 pilots and more than 200 technicians to man two Libyan MiG-23-squadrons based at Benina AB, outside Benghazi. Another similar agreement was reached with North Korea, which

Libya purchased at least 230 Aermacchi SF.260WL training aircraft and light strikes. The majority of these served with the Air Force Academy at Misurata and with advanced training units, but the aircraft subsequently saw extensive combat service during early Libyan interventions in Chad. (Albert Grandolini Collection)

To the surprise of many LAAF officers, the Soviets delivered MiG-23Ms compatible only with entirely obsolete R-3S missiles, four of which can be seen on underwing and under-fuselage weapons of this example, despite availability of more advanced R-13M air-to-air missiles. The Libyans had to adapt the type of carriage of latest weapons locally. (USN)

The MiG-23MS caused immense problems to the FLAAF and took years to introduce to service. This clandestinely taken photograph from early 1975 shows one of first examples delivered to Libya. Notably, as of that time the LAAF was still using pan-Arabic national markings, with its MiG-23s wearing their roundels below the cockpit, as opposed to Egyptian examples that received them on the intake, and Syrian, which received no roundels on the fuselage. (Tom Cooper Collection)

deployed around 100 pilots and technicians to fly LAAF MiG-21s in period 1979–1981.

Although bolstering the number of operational aircraft, in practice this decision caused even more chaos and confusion within the air force and made even routine training operations a complex issue. Namely, by that time the LAAF included: its old but small cadre of US-trained pilots; increasing numbers of novice pilots trained either in Yugoslavia or at the academy in Misurata according to Yugoslav training plans; some pilots trained with the help of Egyptian and Pakistani instructors in Libya; and additional pilots trained in Egypt, France, Romania, the USSR and elsewhere abroad. This resulted in Libyan pilots not only receiving very diverse levels of education, qualifications, and skill, but also 'flying' in several different languages, including English, French, Russian, and, in the case of Syrians, in Arabic. Pilots trained in France found it complicated to cooperate with primarily English-speaking pilots trained elsewhere and very soon it turned out that the quality of training provided by the Soviets was well below the expected level. While it appeared to foreigners that by the mid-1970s Libya's foreign policy had 'tilted dramatically toward increased cooperation with the Soviet Union', in reality, numerous problems developed between Tripoli and Moscow. Many of these were related to deliveries of the MiG-23s. Abdoul Hassan, one of the early Libyan MiG-23-pilots, recalled as follows about the aircraft that was expected to form the backbone of the air force well into the 1980s:

The Soviets announced the MiG-23 as outmatching everything,

their own MiG-21, French Mirage, US-made F-4 Phantom and even the F-14 Tomcat, but delivered only the variant equipped with the weapons system and avionics of the MiG-21. We expected a lot from it but were greatly disappointed during our conversion courses. Essentially, the MiG-23 proved very complex in maintenance and operations. The wing moving mechanism could set the wing to three pre-programmed positions: 16 degrees for slow speed, 45 degrees for combat, and 72 degrees for high-speed flying. Each of these settings changed the flight characteristics dramatically. It was like flying three different aircraft. To fly the MiG-23 you had to be able to fly it well in all three set-ups. The wing moving mechanism was troublesome to maintain. It was made of one big piece of steel, the manufacturing quality of which was poor and it was easy to damage by flying too fast at high speeds and low level. Such flying could also easily damage the cockpit hood, which had to be frequently replaced. We lost several pilots in crashes caused by failures of wing moving mechanisms (and a few to failures of the cockpit hood). Several crashed during practice strafing runs. From that time onwards, our technicians always had an eye on that mechanism.

The next problem was manoeuvring the aircraft in air combat. In manoeuvre, the MiG-23MS and the MiG-23UB had a big problem at a high angle-of-attack (AoA). They were easy to fly outside the envelope and prone to flat spin if pulled above the limit of 24 degrees. There was no AoA-limiter. While flying tight manoeuvres, the pilot had to carefully watch the AoA indicator, not track his target, and tracking the opponent was further problematic because of very poor visibility out of the cockpit, limited by heavy framing.

Another weak spot was the engine. Once the wings of a MiG-23MS were fully swept back, its acceleration was exceptional. Re-trimming the plane was no problem but adjusting power was, because of the engine. The R-29 could accelerate to the point of disintegration, but could not decelerate under the pilot's control. Above Mach 1, there was no response to the throttle, but the pilot had to let the engine decelerate on its own. Combined, all these problems made the MiG-23 very dangerous to fly for our inexperienced pilots. We lost pilots trying to land MiG-23UBs alone because they forgot to move their wings forward, to the minimum position.

The weapons system was also a problem. It included only the old and unreliable R-3S [AA-2 Atoll] air-to-air missiles. What amazed us was that at the time the Soviets were delivering much more advanced R-13M [AA-2c Atoll] missiles together with

Gaddafi with members of the RCC and top military commanders during planning for first operations against Egypt in 1976. (Gaddafi Collection)

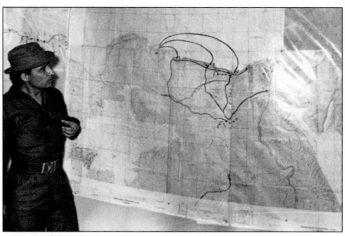

One of the Libyan officers in front of a map clearly showing the Gamal Abdel Nasser AB and air strikes planned to be flown by LAAF Mirages against targets well inside Egypt. (Gaddafi Collection)

MiG-21bis to us. We decided to re-wire our MiG-23MS to match them with R-13Ms. During the test-firing of this weapon another catastrophe occurred. When fired from one of the hardpoints under the fuselage, the smoke from R-13M entered the engine and caused it to malfunction. The plane fell into the spin and our test pilot barely survived. This experience forced us to modify only underwing hardpoints to carry R-13Ms.

Persistent problems with MiG-23MS's caused much frustration within the LAAF, bringing its cooperation with the Soviets to the brink of collapse. The situation did not improve once the first MiG-23BNs entered service, as explained by Hassan:

The MiG-23BN was a dedicated ground-attack variant, designed for fast and straight flying at low altitude, where it offered a smooth ride. Early on we experienced the same maintenance problems as with MiG-23MS's and lost a number of pilots and aircraft. Some crashed due to failures of the wing moving mechanism, others due to engine failures, and there were pilot errors too. Once the problems were solved, this variant turned into a true workhorse and could be flown intensively. Like other MiG-23-variants, the MiG-23BN came with capability to deploy the Kh-23 guided missile. Unlike MiG-23MS's, it did not need to carry the Delta guidance pod, it had this installed in the right wing root. However, the Kh-23 was a big disappointment, very unreliable and thus seldom used. Instead, we always armed our MiG-23BNs with bombs like FAB-250 and -500, OFAB-100, ZAB-350 and -500 napalm bombs, UB-16-57 pods for unguided rockets calibre 57mm and others.

Hazem al-Bajigni's early experience with MiG-23 was not much different:

I was sent to the USSR in 1976 for a conversion course on MiG-23BN, together with ten other pilots. Due to a disagreement over the nature of our program things did not go well, and we returned a few months later. Hardly back from the Soviet Union, I then experienced a very nasty accident in a MiG-23UB. We lost the hydraulic system and Natasha (vocal alarm system) was blurting all sorts of warnings. I ejected my Russian instructor and me at high, negative g-forces and we were both blinded for three days. We were rescued by some Bedouins that put us in a Toyota Land Cruiser and subsequently I was sent to West Germany for medical treatment.

Eventually, training of Libyan pilots in the USSR was discontinued in 1977 and subsequently it was primarily more experienced Syrians that flew MiG-23MS interceptors. The LAAF demanded that the Soviets rectify all technical issues with the aircraft, as recalled by Hussein:

We insisted the Soviets correct all the problems and repair our MiG-23s. We paid them millions for aircraft that were poorly manufactured and that malfunctioned all the time. They put all the blame upon us. They said our technicians were lazy and did not follow the prescribed maintenance routines, our pilots could not fly and were ejecting from their aircraft at the first sign of problems, and many, many other things. At the same time they would not even provide us with spares, tools and technical documentation to maintain our aircraft.

Despite protracted 'negotiations' (not a few of which ended on the brink of fist-fights) no solution for the issue was found. With average operational rates for MiG-23s dropping to less than 50%, the LAAF found itself preoccupied spending years introducing the aircraft to service, although in the opinion of many, it was simply not worth the money. Eventually, the Libyans turned to entirely unexpected parties for help, as recalled by Bajigni:

With no end of problems with MiG-23 in sight, we felt forced to hire a few experienced American and Pakistani pilots to test-fly our MiG-23s and to help re-write their flight manuals. Of course, the Russians were furiously mad when they heard about this.

It was because of such experiences that the LAAF subsequently contracted the Yugoslav company Zmaj from Velika Gorica, near Zagreb (since 1991 the capital of Croatia), to overhaul its MiG-21bis's, instead of sending them to the USSR for maintenance, again causing outraged protests from Moscow.

Of course, there was no similar solution for the problem related to the integration of pilots trained in different countries within the LAAF. The solution of allotting each of these groups a different slot of training time or grouping them at different bases, proved anything but satisfactory. On the contrary, this issue became even more problematic due to several coup attempts against Gaddafi launched from within the military. The most serious of these was plotted in 1975 by two members of the RCC in cooperation with 30 army officers, and resulted in the purge of a number of top

Formation of Egyptian Su-20 swing-wing fighter-bombers, as used for the final attack on Gamal Abdel Nasser AB on the morning of 24 July 1977. (Albert Grandolini Collection)

Wreckage of an Egyptian fighter-bomber, claimed as shot down by LAAF Mirages near GANAB in July 1977. If Egyptian accounts about this short conflict are correct, this was the Su-7BMK flown by Major Mohammad Ifaat, shot down during the afternoon of 21 July. (via Tom Cooper)

Group of Egyptian PoWs captured by Libyans during the July 1977 War. (Gaddafi Collection)

ranking commanders as well as other solutions designed to prevent the creation of 'cliques' within the military. The measures in question only increased problems with unit cohesion and, together with the latent inexperience of top commanders, the inability of the entire LAAF to operate effectively. Eventually, it took the top Libyan military commanders several first-hand, and usually very unpleasant, combat experiences in order to start sorting out the entire mess they had created.

Disastrous War with Egypt

Relations between Egypt and Libya continued to deteriorate during the period 1974–1976, because President Sadat entered peace negotiations with Israel. From Gaddafi's standpoint, this was entirely unacceptable; he accused Sadat of betraying the Arab cause and began supporting opposition groups in Egypt in attempt to incite popular unrest. As mutual accusations and offence flew in both directions, the Libyan army provoked a number of border clashes, prompting the Egyptians to re-deploy two mechanised infantry divisions into the area in 1976. Gaddafi ordered several mechanised battalions with about 4,000 troops and 150 tanks and armoured cars to the border but tensions swiftly dissipated. Preoccupied with negotiations with Israel and economic difficulties caused by Egypt continuously fighting Israel for nearly a decade, Sadat was keen to

avoid getting his country involved in another war. Furthermore, the Egyptian Army had neither planned nor rehearsed for any kind of war with Libya, and it lacked the necessary infrastructure to support such an effort. For the Egyptian Army and Air Force to operate effectively, all the necessary work had first to be undertaken by the Egyptian General Staff, and this required several months to prepare contingency plans. This process was completed only during early summer 1977, when the EAF was ordered to start distributing its Sukhoi Su-7s and Sukhoi Su-20s from No. 55 Squadron, plus Mirage 5s from No. 69 Squadron to Marsa Matruh AB and nearby airfields.[26] Major Ahmed Abbas flew MiG-21s with another unit ordered to face Libya, Air Brigade 111, and recalled having mixed feelings:

We had been based at Cairo West ever since the end of the October 1973 War with Israel. In the summer 1976, we were suddenly ordered to re-deploy to Jiyanklis AB, near Alexandria and to prepare for intensive exercises. Four days after moving there, and after flying lots of training sorties, we received a briefing to prepare for a war with Libya. For us it was unexpected and hard to understand why we should fight a friendly Muslim country. But any problems with morale were solved as soon as we had been informed that Libyans were frequently violating our airspace and the territorial integrity of our country, killing a number of our border guards.[27]

After apparently learning about the plan from their sympathisers in Cairo, the Soviets warned Libya that they had reliable evidence of Egyptian preparations for a major invasion of Libya in May 1977.

26 This time the Mirages operated by Egyptians did not come from Libya: Libyan Mirages were all returned in 1974. On the contrary, the aircraft in question included 32 Mirage 5SDE interceptors and fighter-bombers, ordered by Saudi Arabia on behalf of Egypt, in July 1972. They wore markings of the Royal Saudi Air Force until their delivery to Egypt, in 1974, where they were used to replace Libyan Mirages operated until then by the No. 69 Squadron. Egypt subsequently continued ordering additional Mirages from France, including 14 Mirage 5SDE-2s in 1974, 8 in 1977, and 16 Mirage M5 E2 fighter-bombers in 1982. While majority of SDE-2s entered service with No. 71 Squadron, M5 E2s were used to equip the newly-established No. 73 Squadron. These units were reinforced through addition of six Mirage 5SDR reconnaissance fighters and six Mirage 5SDD two-seat conversion trainers, ordered in 1982 too (see Beaumont, pp. 44–45, 69 & 78).
27 Abbas, interview to Group 73, Apr. 2013; this and all subsequent quotations from Abbas are based on transcription of the same interview.

Pre-delivery photograph of one of around 36 Su-22s (note the large housing for a laser-ranger underneath the intake) purchased by Libya in the late 1970s. It seems that most of these aircraft received additional splotches of dark green colour by the time they entered service with No. 1032 and No. 1036 Squadrons LAAF. (Robert Szombati Collection)

Following negative experiences with the training of its MiG-23-pilots in the USSR, the LAAF purchased a small number of MiG-25PU conversion trainers and these were used to train Libyan pilots to fly and operate the aircraft in Libya. This example was operated by No. 1035 Squadron from Um Aittitiqah AB, where it was photographed in abandoned condition in 2009. (Photo by Eddy de Krujif)

Gaddafi touring Um Aittitiqah AB together with Yassir Arafat, the leader of the Palestinian Liberation Organization, in front of a LAAF MiG-25RB serial number 486 in 1980. (Gaddafi Collection)

This MiG-25P serial number 903 was one of around fifteen examples of this variant operated by No. 1035 Squadron during the 1980s and 1990s. (Photo by Eddy de Krujif)

Bajigni recalled Gaddafi's reaction to the Egyptians massing their units along the border as follows:

> Colonel Farijani ill-advised our War Council. He massively exaggerated the effectiveness of our air force. He bragged that we could defeat the EAF within a few days of intensive operations and open the way to Cairo. Sure, we did have the machinery and even the manpower by that time, but not the experience. And the Egyptians knew a lot about us and our capabilities from their earlier cooperation with us.

Indeed, the RCC ordered the army to renew small-scale border raids, some of which turned into hour-long fire fights between battalion-sized forces, on 12 and 16 July 1977.[28] By that time, the balance of forces was still heavily against the Libyans; their entire military still totalled barely 40,000 officers and other ranks, and only some 5,000, organised into six battalions, were deployed along the border with Egypt. Although the LAAF had an entire squadron operational with Mirage IIIR reconnaissance fighters, Libyan commanders possessed next to no ability to properly utilise them or analyse enemy dispositions and therefore react to the intelligence they could obtain. Unsurprisingly, when the Libyan 9th Tank

28 Pollack, pp. 363–364.

Battalion launched another raid against the Egyptian border town of as-Sallum on 21 July, it ran straight into an ambush set up by an entire Egyptian division. After suffering nearly fifty percent losses, the survivors of the unit fell back in disarray and the army called in the LAAF for help.

In theory, Farijani could call upon more than 100 Mirages and 100 MiG-23s by that time. However, due to problems with MiG-23s, only Mirage equipped units and training squadrons at Misurata were ready, and only Mirages of the GANAB-based No. 1002 Squadron appeared over as-Sallum during the afternoon of 21 July. They caused little damage, and the Egyptians claimed two of them as shot down by ground fire, including one by SA-7 MANPADs.

Considering the involvement of the LAAF in this provocation, the Egyptians decided to respond. Later in the afternoon Colonel Adil Nassr, one of the most senior Egyptian officers when UARAF units were based in Libya and now commander of EAF units based at Marsa Matruh, received the order to attack the Gamal Abdel Nasser Air Base, south of Tobruk. He assembled his squadron commanders and ordered them into action, as recalled by Abbas:

> Our order was to send eight Su-7s (one flight led by Mohi al-Noor, the other by Kamal Abdel), and four Mirages into an attack on that base. Four MiG-21s were to provide top cover, but two of Mirages were armed with air-to-air missiles too. Other fighter-bombers attacked Libyan radar stations in Bardiyah and al-Jaghbūb to blind Libyan air defences. We flew from Marsa Matruh in a westerly direction along a specially designed corridor within

Considering them as 'Soviet flown' and thus a serious threat to NATO's 'southern flank', various US intelligence agencies carefully monitored the introduction to service of Tu-22 bombers in Libya. This LAAF Tu-22A (ASCC code 'Blinder-B') was intercepted by two F-4s of the US Navy's VF-51 Squadron over the Mediterranean Sea in early 1977 (VF-51 was assigned to CVW-19 and embarked on board the USS *F. D. Roosevelt (CV-42)* at that time). (USN)

LAAF Lt Saleh Sharif Abdul Wafi with a Mirage 5D of No. 1002 Squadron in November 1978. (via Ali Tani)

our air defences. We saw Tobruk clearly from far away and then turned left to attack. The Su-7s encountered heavy air defences, and the plane flown by Major Mohammad Ifaat was shot down in flames. Mirages achieved very good results, hitting several aircraft parked on the tarmac. Later that evening the Libyans dragged Ifaat in front of their TV cameras. They had beaten him badly and some even extinguished their cigarettes on his body. They forced him to make anti-Egyptian statements to the press. That was very unfortunate.

Contrary to the usual Western reports, which stress that the EAF attack caused next to no or only light damage, not only did the Egyptian pilots claim seven aircraft hits on the ground, the recollections of Libyan pilots show that this strike was highly effective. In Bajigni's words:

> For some strange reason, Farijani ordered more than 20 Galebs and Jastrebs from the Academy in Misurata to re-deploy to Nasser Air Base. Nearly all of them were destroyed on the ground. We did shoot down one Egyptian Su-7 and captured the pilot, but this deployment ended in a disastrous fashion.[29]

While available sources disagree whether Captain Ifaat's Su-7 was shot down by a LAAF Mirage or ground-based air defences, as far as Egyptian sources go this was the only fighter-bomber the EAF lost over Libya. However, former Yugoslav instructors serving at Misurata recalled differently:

> During the war we were ordered to prepare our aircraft for combat, but fortunately the war was very short and there was no need for us to fly combat sorties against the Egyptians. The Soviets had a large group of instructors deployed in Libya helping establish the local air defences. Glad to prove the effectiveness of their weapons, but also because the Egyptians kicked them out of their bases, the Soviets were very eager for a payback. The Egyptians attacked the Nasser AB several times and destroyed neat rows of

Libyan aircraft on the ground, but the Soviets manning Libyan air defences shot down many of them in return.[30]

Irrespectively of whether the EAF suffered additional losses or not, after knocking out about 60 Libyan main battle tanks (MBTs), armoured cars and APCs, during the evening of 21 July, the Egyptian ground forces withdrew back across the border. Obviously satisfied by finding out that the opposition was only lightly armed and tended to flee after suffering losses, Sadat did not want to persevere.

Still under the impression of Farijani's advice, Gaddafi continued the action and early the next morning LAAF Mirages flew sixteen low-level strikes against Egyptian ground forces in the as-Sallum area. Egyptian air defences claimed two fighter-bombers as shot down, and Tripoli confirmed the loss, but insisted that one was hit by Libyan air defences and the other crashed during a reconnaissance sortie. As could be expected, the Egyptians were keen to curb Libyan aerial operations, and the CO of the Su-20-equipped No. 55 Squadron, Lt Col Mohammed al-Ibrahim, received an order to fly another strike against GANAB. Flown by eight Sukhois, this mission was successful in putting the major LAAF base in eastern Libya out of commission for the rest of 22 July 1977. The Egyptians exploited this opportunity by launching heliborne commando attacks on additional radar sites, forward storage depots and military facilities in al-Kufra and al-Jaghbüb, and even several training camps for Egyptian dissidents, during the following night.

Despite heavy losses at GANAB, the LAAF returned to the skies on the morning of 23 July, its Mirages flying low over the Mediterranean Sea before turning south to attack targets well inside Egypt, including Mersa Matruh AB. Their operations were supported by Mil Mi-8 helicopters equipped for emitting electronic-countermeasures, which did have some effect on the capability of Egyptian Air Defence Command to control the skies along the border and the coast. However, the effects of jamming were decreased by EAF MiG-21s flying near continuous combat air patrols down the threat axis, and during the day Egyptian pilots and air defences claimed four Mirages as shot down. Finally, on the morning of 24 July, EAF Su-20s hit GANAB for the third time, cratering both runways with Egyptian-designed and manufactured runway penetrating bombs. Shortly after, president Sadat ordered the end of Egyptian operations and a unilateral cease-fire. Although

29 The Libyan version of the results of this attack, provided to authors in 2006, was independently confirmed by Mohammad al-Ibrahim in interview to Lon Nordeen, Cairo, Apr. 1999.

30 Sinisa Klarica, 'Gadafi nije bio pitomac u Zemuniku' ('Gaddafi was no Cadet in Zemunik', in Croatian), *Zadarski List*, 24 Feb. 2011.

Table 1: LAAF Order of Battle, 1970–1985

Unit	Aircraft Type	Base	Notes
No.1001 Squadron	Mirage 5D	Ukba Ibn Nafi	operational in 1971–2003 period; aircraft subsequently stored
No.1002 Squadron	Mirage 5D	Ukba Ibn Nafi	
No.1003 Squadron	Mirage 5DE	Ukba Ibn Nafi	operational 1971–1979; subsequent status unclear
No.1004 Squadron	Mirage 5R	Ukba Ibn Nafi	operational 1971–1989; subsequent status unclear
No.1005 Squadron	MiG-25P, MiG-25PU	al-Jufra/Hun	Operational Conversion Unit
No.1010 Squadron	MiG-23MS, MiG-23UB, MiG-23BN	Misurata	training unit
No.1011 Squadron	Mirage F.1AD	Ukba Ibn Nafi	
No.1012 Squadron	Mirage F.1ED	Ukba Ibn Nafi	also known as 'Fatah Squadron'
No.1015 Squadron	MiG-25P	Ukba Ibn Nafi	
No.1020 Squadron	G-2 Galeb	Misurata	element of LAAF Academy
No.1021 Squadron	MiG-21bis/UM	GANAB	
No.1022 Squadron	Tu-22A/U	al-Jufra/Hun	
No.1023 Squadron	MiG-23MS/UB	Umm Aittitiqah/Mitiga	
No.1024 Squadron	MiG-23MS/UB	unknown	
No.1025 Squadron	MiG-25	al-Jufra/Hun	
No.1030 Squadron	Mirage 5DD	Ukba Ibn Nafi	Operational Conversion Unit
No.1032 Squadron	Su-22, Su-22M/M-2K	Syrte/Ghurdabiyah	
No.1035 Squadron	MiG-25P/R	Umm Aittitiqah/Mitiga	
No.1036 Squadron	Su-22, Su-22M/M-2K	Syrte/Ghurdabiyah	
No. 1039 Squadron	L-39ZO	Umm Aittitiqah/Mitiga	
No.1040 Squadron	MiG-23MS/UB	Benina/Benghazi	
No.1042 Squadron	Su-22		supposedly established at Ghadames, but never confirmed as operational
No. 1050 Squadron	MiG-23MS/UB	Benina/Benghazi	manned by SyAAF, 1977–1982
No. 1055 Squadron	MiG-25		planned but never officially established
No. 1060 Squadron	MiG-23BN/UB	Benina/Benghazi	manned by SyAAF, 1977–1982
No. 1070 Squadron	MiG-23BN/UB	al-Abraq	
No. 1160 Squadron	SF.260WL	Ma'arten as-Sahra	COIN unit established for operations in Chad
No. 1222 Squadron	G.222T	Benina/Benghazi	
No. 1226 Squadron	An-26	Umm Aittitiqah/Mitiga	
No. 1240 Squadron	JetStar, Learjet	Tripoli IAP	
No. 130? Squadron	Mi-2/-8/-25	Martubah	Operational Conversion Unit
No. 1308 Squdron	Mi-8	Ukba Ibn Nafi	
No. 1316 Squadron	SA.316B Alouette III	Tripoli IAP	
No. 1321 Squadron	SA.321 Super Frelon		
No. 1325 Squadron	Mi-25		
No. 1347 Squadron	CH-47C	Umm Aittitiqah/Mitiga	

some small-scale fighting continued for the next few days, for all practical purposes the short Egyptian–Libyan War thus ended after three days of intensive operations.

Salleh's Modernisation Push
In the course of the war with Egypt the LAAF lost up to twenty Galebs and Jastrebs, six Mirages and several radar stations, while the Libyan Army was forced to write off more than 80 armoured vehicles and several artillery batteries. Nearly all of the Libyan military bases

between Tobruk and the border with Egypt had suffered various degrees of damage as the EAF established aerial supremacy over the battlefield. Certainly, the Egyptians lacked the firepower to cause decisive damage, and the political will to widen the conflict through large-scale operations. They also suffered a number of losses of aircraft and personnel, and even had some of their troops captured by the Libyans. However, Sadat's sole intention was to 'send a message' to Tripoli, and this is precisely what his armed forces did. Understanding that his military was too hopelessly outclassed

Unknown in the West, Libyan-Soviet relations suffered a lot due to the 'MiG-23-affair' of the late 1970s. It took major efforts by Col Saleh and several visits of Soviet leader Leonid Brezhnev to repair this friendship. (Gaddafi Collection)

Libya acquired at least thirteen Antonov An-26 transports in 1979. (Albert Grandolini Collection)

The LAAF purchased twenty G.222Ts from Italy, of which two were equipped as VIP-transports. Powered by Rolls Royce Tine turboprops, they served with No. 1222 Squadron based at Benina AB starting from 1983. (Albert Grandolini Collection)

and out of condition to instigate any kind of political changes in Cairo, Gaddafi subsequently gave up his pressure upon Egypt. Furthermore, dissatisfied with Farijani's performance, he dismissed the LAAF commander and replaced him with another US-trained officer (and former CH-47-pilot), Col Salleh Abdullah Salleh.

Salleh attempted to solve the problems the air force was facing through initiatives in several different directions. He re-established ties with Moscow and, following extensive negotiations, ordered additional advanced aircraft. The first of these were at least 36 Sukhoi Su-22 and Su-22M fighter-bombers, which began arriving in 1978. The Sukhois were followed by the first batch of 60 MiG-25P interceptors and MiG-25R reconnaissance fighters capable of reaching speeds of Mach 3 at altitudes of 21,000m (68,900ft) and higher. Despite the availability of several sources, the service history of both of these aircraft in Libya largely remains obscure and when encountered by foreign air forces, primarily US Navy pilots, for the first time, there was plenty of guessing about them being flown by Soviet pilots. Ali Tani underwent a conversion course for the MiG-25 in 1978:

> After doing post-delivery test-flights, Soviet pilots never flew any Libyan MiG-25s. There were Soviet instructors in Libya, but only to help us in training and the working up of our units. They were not permitted to live on our air base, they lived in a hotel nearby, from which they could only move escorted by guards. The Soviets became involved in several attempts at smuggling liquor and gold, and often got themselves into problems with our customs. The initial plan was for the LAAF to establish six squadrons equipped with MiG-25s, including Nos. 1005, 1010, 1015, 1025, 1035 and 1055. Four units became operational by 1981, No. 1005 and 1025 at al-Jufra/Hun, No. 1015 at UINAB [Ukba Ibn Nafi AB], and No. 1035 at Mitiga. The latter unit included a reconnaissance detachment equipped with six MiG-25Rs. Stocks of spares and maintenance facilities were established at Sebha. All units had regular detachments deployed at Misurata and Benina.

Only one Libyan MiG-25 is known to have crashed during the conversion course for the first group of LAAF pilots, on 21 November 1978, once again prompting Western reports that the type was flown by Soviet pilots.[31] Actually, the aircraft in question was a Libyan owned MiG-25PU two-seat conversion trainer that, according to Tani, suffered an engine malfunction forcing the crew to eject. Sadly, one of them drowned after landing in the sea, some 100km north-west of Tripoli.

The Su-22 and the Su-22Ms (some of which might have been upgraded to Su-22M-2K standard by 1981) were very good fighter-bombers, described by Libyan pilots as 'stable, safe and comfortable aircraft to fly'. While having no radar and only a self-defence capability in the form of two R-3S or R-13M air-to-air missiles, they were compatible with a range of TV and laser-guided missiles, and anti-radar missiles. In the words of one former LAAF pilot, 'they had a very good RWR and could do a lots of things the MiG-23BN was unable to do'.

Meanwhile, the LAAF also received the first Tu-22A bombers. The aircraft in question were in reality second-hand, Tu-22RDs operated by the Soviet Air Force since the mid-1960s. Before their delivery, they had their reconnaissance equipment removed and were overhauled. Libyan crews then underwent conversion courses at Zyabrovka AB and at the 147th School at Savostleyka AB starting in late 1973. The first three Libyan Tu-22 pilots are said to have been Colonel Masun (or Masood) Mathelon, Captain Akil Za'tari and Lt Mohammad Kabalan. As far as is known, their Soviet instructors were less than impressed by the performance of LAAF pilots, rating most of them only as 'fair', complaining about their lack of aggressiveness and that they did not master tactical weapons delivery

---

31 A report in *Flight* Magazine, on 2 Dec. 1978, stated: 'Originally based in Egypt, the Foxbat detachment moved out when President Sadat expelled the large Soviet training mission prior to the 1973 Yom Kippur War. Syria was the next temporary home, but political pressures prompted a move to Libya…'

methods but were passed for political reasons. Their conclusion was that Libyan Tu-22-crews would be barely capable of executing even short-duration missions on the aircraft and that their combat operations would always be driven by self-preservation rather than the task on hand. However, as time would tell, Libyan Tu-22 operations were foremost to suffer from exactly the same problem that dogged that aircraft's service in the USSR: serviceability. The aircraft was a handful to maintain and fly. Particular problems were posed by the maintenance of the RD7-M2 engines, which were positioned high above the fuselage and thus exceptionally problematic to reach for technicians. The engines were also causing problems for pilots who had to pay careful attention to very precise throttle settings. Any mistake during flight would easily lead to an engine malfunction, which, especially at supersonic speeds, regularly resulted in a disintegration of the airframe. While offering impressive performance for a plane of its size and weight, the Tu-22 was difficult to fly at high speeds and notorious for its high landing speed of 310km/h (192mph). A breaking chute was vital for a safe landing; the loss or malfunction of this usually meant the loss of the aircraft and the the crew, as there was no way of stopping the Tu-22 even on the longest runway using only brakes, and the ejection seats of the co-pilot and navigator fired downwards. Despite experiencing extensive problems with the aircraft, the LAAF gradually worked up No. 1022 Squadron, half of which (sometimes reported as 'Second Bomber Squadron') was a dedicated training outfit.[32] Even as of 1977, a full two years after the aircraft officially entered service, not all the aircraft were delivered, additional crews were still undergoing training in the USSR (a process that was to last until 1983 at least),

---

32 Alternative reports indicate that the LAAF actually established two small units equipped with Tu-22s, including Nos. 1110 and 1120 Squadron. However, this remains unconfirmed and it seems that only one unit ever became operational, designated as the No. 1022 Squadron.

and only three or four bombers could be maintained in operational condition on average. The main base of this unit was the newly constructed al-Jufra/Hun AB in central Libya, but detachments were regularly deployed at UINAB and Umm Aititiiqah AB, while the main stock of spares was positioned at Ghadames AB, a situation that certainly did not help routine maintenance.

Except for acquiring more potent combat aircraft, the LAAF further expanded its transport fleet through acquisitions of Ilyushin Il-76M and Il-76TD, and Antonov An-26 transports from the USSR, and Aeritalia G.222T transports ordered from Italy in 1981. During the late 1970s and early 1980s the helicopter fleet was vastly expanded too, primarily through purchases of Mil Mi-8 transport helicopters and Mi-25 helicopter gunships of Soviet origin.

The next step in the development of the LAAF was to become the establishment of wing structure, each of which was to consist of two or three squadrons concentrated at the same air base. Although the relevant orders are known to have been issued and some of the related work done, this process was never completed, and not a single wing of the Libyan Air Force is known to have ever been officially established. Apparently, a combination of Gaddafi's decreasing trust in his military, reinforced by a series of coup-attempts, and increasing interest in other affairs, combined with decreasing income from petrochemical products and Soviet refusal to provide more advanced aircraft, led to the loss of interest in further investment in the air force. This resulted in continuous lack of trained and qualified personnel, which in turn resulted in a situation where the LAAF never had more than about twenty operational squadrons at one time. Although hundreds of additional pilots and ground crews underwent training in the late 1970s and early 1980s, many of units listed in Table 1, which summarises the composition of the Libyan air force during this period, were almost continuously under their authorised strength.

CHAPTER 3
CHADIAN PREQUEL

Except for his attempts to unite Libya with Egypt and Syria, during the 1970s Gaddafi attempted to merge Libya with a number of other Arab and African countries, including Tunisia, Sudan, Algeria, and Morocco. All his attempts were unsuccessful, usually for the same reason: while the Libyan leader was insisting on immediate action, other Arab statesmen preferred a gradual process. Every time his attempts failed, convinced of the righteousness of his cause, Gaddafi reverted to nonconventional methods, primarily subversion, support of coup attempts plotted by local military and security forces and, in extreme cases, also sponsoring international terrorism. In 1971, King Hassan II of Morocco accused Libya of supporting a coup attempt against him, although this was staged by his Minister of Defence and top officers of the Royal Moroccan Air Force for exactly the same reasons Gaddafi and his comrades staged the coup against King Idris II. In 1974, President Habib Bourguiba of Tunisia accused Gaddafi of instigating acts of subversion, including plots to assassinate government officials that opposed a union between the two countries and attempts to incite armed rebellion. Tunisia was to find itself on the receiving end of one Libyan-supported invasion, six years later.

Furthermore, Gaddafi sought to spread his influence into Sub-Saharan Africa and thus established close ties to several local rulers. That is how the Libyan military became involved in Uganda in 1972, but especially during the so-called Kagera War between Uganda and Tanzania between 1978 and 1979, which is to become a topic of a future volume in the Africa@War series. However, nowhere did Gaddafi go as far as in the case of Libya's southern neighbour, Chad.

Libyan involvement in that country dated back to the times of King Idris II's rule, and was initially related to tribal ties between people living on either side of the mutual border. Libyan claims for the Aouzou Strip in northern Chad were based on a treaty made by Vichy France with Mussolini during World War II. However, Idris never became as deeply involved in local affairs as Gaddafi, whose designs went well beyond a 'union' of the two countries.

Chadian Independence
Chad is a land-locked country in northern central Africa that gained independence from France on 11 August 1960. N'Djamena (Fort Lamy until 1972) is the capital and largest city. Ever since independence, this sparsely populated country that is two times the

M3 armoured personnel carriers of the ANT, as seen during a military parade in Fort Lamy in the 1960s. (Albert Grandolini Collection)

size of France, has been plagued by political instability and internal unrest, armed uprisings, foreign invasions, and outright banditry.

The terrain of Chad is dominated by the low-lying Chad Basin, which rises gradually to mountains and plateaus in the east (900 metre high Ennedi and Oueddei Plateaus), and the north, where the greatest elevations are reached in the Tibesti massif (3,415m high Emi Koussi). The northern part of the country lies in the Sahara and is dominated by a vast, hot and arid desert. The central section of the country has three seasons: hot from March to July; rainy from July to October; and cool during the remaining months. The southern section has similar seasons but receives more rainfall and includes the only important rivers, the Logone and Chari (or Shair), both of which flow into Lake Chad, which doubles in size during the rainy season. Although only 3% of the land is cultivated, agriculture remains of primary importance for food production, together with extensive fish resources in Lake Chad and the Chari River. While Natron (sodium carbonate) used to be the only mineral extracted in significant quantities in the past, deposits of petroleum were discovered near Lake Chad, and uranium in the north in more recent times, and these appear to have been exploited by the Chinese and French under quite secretive circumstances.

Cave paintings indicate that Chad was a fertile and populous country in ancient times, but very little is known about its history before the 9th century AD, when the Kingdom of Kanem was established in what is now western Chad, with its capital at Njimi, near Mao. Its rulers adopted Islam in the 11th century. Kanem was subsequently subjected to neighbouring Bornu in the 16th century, and then to the sultanates of Baguirmi and Wadai in the south, before coming under the rule of the Sudanese conqueror Rabih az-Zubyar in the 19th century and ending under the French rule, upon az-Zubayr's death and the battle of Kousseri, in 1900. Ten years later, Chad was declared a part of the French Equatorial Federation, but the fact that this was administered from Brazzaville (nowadays the capital of the Republic of Congo) meant that the life of the indigenous people experienced very little interference. While only French and Arabic are considered official languages, the modern-day population of Chad is diverse, consisting of six major ethnic groups distributed in about 250 clans and tribes, some of which speak different African languages, including Hausa in the Lake Chad area. Essentially, the population is divided into two main groups. Approximately 50% of the population are Muslims,

including indigenous groups of Arabs, Toubou, Hadjerai, Fulani, Fulbe, Kotoko, Kanembou, Baguirmi, Boulala, and Maba. Another Muslim group is the Zaghawa tribe that, according to the locals, primarily consists of late-comers that moved in from Sudan in the early 1960s, but especially in the 1970s. Several other indigenous groups, such as the Salamat and the Taundjor, were largely Arabised by intermarriage over the years. Muslims predominantly live in the northern and eastern portions of the country. The largest single group in Chad are the Sara, which make up about 30% of the population and are predominantly Christians, living in the south.

The National Chadian Armed Forces (Armée Nationale du Tchad, ANT) were formed from Chadian veterans of the French Army, and inherited stock of French arms and equipment. A bilateral military technical assistance agreement provided additional equipment and some 500 French officers and other ranks to serve as advisers and instructors. The same agreement provided France also with base rights, transit and overflight privileges, and the right to assist the ANT in issues related to internal security. A contingent of about 900 French troops controlled northern Chad until 1965, and made good use of Fort Lamy for interventions in Congo-Brazzaville in 1963, Gabon in 1964 and in Chad through subsequent years. By 1968 the ANT was expanded in size to about 1,200 officers, non commissioned officers (NCOs) and other ranks. These were organised into six infantry companies and one airborne company, all grouped within the same regiment that also operated a number of obsolete M8 armoured cars and M5 half-tracks. There was also a 700-man strong Gendarmerie (Constabulary), and a National Guard operated by the Ministry of Internal Affairs, primarily made up of nomadic companies, mounted on camels and horses. This force was supported by a 120-men strong French military mission, many of whom were involved in training a small flying branch that by 1969 consisted of five C-47s and three Max Holste MH.1521 Broussard liaison aircraft. As of that time, there was only one qualified native pilot, with a few others still in training. Therefore, most aircraft were crewed by the French.

Incipient Insurgency

Relations between the Christians and the Muslims were relatively good until independence, when southerner Francois Tombalbaye, a former teacher and a trade union activist, was declared President of the Republic. Tombalbaye relied heavily upon the French and

Group of FROLINAT insurgents undergoing training in the mid-1960s. With even obsolete rifles left over from World War II, Chadian tribal fighters were poorly armed in the 1960s. (Albert Grandolini Collection)

FROLINAT insurgent armed with a German-made MP40, as photographed in 1968. (Albert Grandolini Collection)

support from his political base in the south, which caused increasing dissent in the north. Beginning in 1963, several opposition movements appeared, primarily amongst Moubi tribesmen at Mangalame (Guera prefecture), but including a number of distinguished persons from the south. While their leaders insisted on complete and 'true' independence from France, the exploitation of national resources in the interest of and to the advantage of local people and respect for the traditional way of life, the majority of tribesmen opposed Tombalbaye's favouring of southerners and his attempts to curb local traditional leaders, as well as widespread corruption and abuses in the process of collecting taxes. Launched from Sudan by a group that armed itself with traditional weapons and an assortment of old World War II arms, the first insurgency failed because the government reacted with harsh repression, killing as many as 500 and forcing all the leaders to flee to Ghana in 1964.[33]

Despite this reversal, the rebellion spread to Bartha Prefecture and then to Oueddei and Salamat. By 22 June 1966, some of the leaders of the first insurgency reorganised various armed groups as the Chadian National Liberation Front (Front de Libération Nationale du Tchad, FROLINAT). Led by Ibrahim Abacha, this force totalled around 3,000 insurgents that began receiving support from several neighbouring Muslim countries, including Algeria and Libya. Still under the rule of King Idris, the government of the latter maintained close relations with several Chadian ethnic groups for familial but also other reasons. The King's bodyguards consisted almost entirely of Toubou tribesmen from Chad, while the king was claiming the Aouzou Strip in northern Chad on the basis of the aforementioned Vichy French–Fascist Italy treaty. However, trying hard to keep himself out of trouble and avoid confrontation with France, Idris limited his support to the provision of food and other supplies to the FROLINAT (but no armament), which mainly operated from bases inside Sudan.

Abacha was killed in a clash with the ANT near Abéche in February 1968, but the FROLINAT structure survived and re-emerged under the leadership of Dr Abba Siddick. A splinter group that became known as the Second Liberation Army FROLINAT,

dominated by the Toubou tribesmen, subsequently emerged in the north of the country, and a third branch, the Third Liberation Army, came into being in Kanem Province under the leadership of Mohmammad Abu Baker Mustafa. The insurgency erupted again on 5 March 1968, when the Second Liberation Army opened its operations in the Borku-Ennedi-Tibesti Prefecture (so-called BET, which represents nearly 45% of total Chadian territory) together with a mutiny of the Toubou-dominated National Guard and Nomad Guard that broke out at the garrison of Aouzou, in August of the same year. This collapsed the government control over the BET, and prompted what gradually developed into the first French intervention in Chad.

French Expeditionary Capability of the 1960s

As of the mid-1960s, the French armed forces were undergoing a process of reorganisation initiated at the end of the Algerian War in 1962. This saw a drastic reduction in defence spending and the disbandment of numerous units in all branches. With the public tired of colonial wars that brought the nation to the verge of a civil war, the era of foreign military interventions appeared to be over. Instead, the government of President Charles De Gaulle distanced the country from NATO and focused all of its intention on revamping the economy through modernisation of industry and investment into new technologies. The emphasis in the future development of the military was focused on the development of nuclear weapons and modernisation of the air force and navy, through the introduction of a new generation of advanced weapons

33 Abubaker Abderahmane, interview, Damascus, Mar. 2006. Abderahmane recalled how the five leaders of the first uprising – including himself, Abu Baker Jalaboo Usman, Ibrahim Abaja, Tahir Mohammad Ali, and Goukouni Oueddei – were motivated by rumours that 'Chad is swimming on the lake of oil', and imagined turning their country into 'another Saudi Arabia'. After the failure of their insurgency, four of them fled to Ghana, while Abderahmane fled to Sudan; only Abderahmane and Oueddei returned to Chad, where they remained until 1982.

The airfield of Mongo in central Chad, one of more than 50 dirt strips constructed by the French during the 1950s and 1960s, as seen from the cockpit of an H-34 in the late 1960s. (Bernard Lart via Arnaud Delalande)

An AD-4N of ELAA.1/22 as seen at Fort Lamy in 1970 or 1971. Of interest is the unit's crest applied on the engine cowling. (S. P. via Arnaud Delalande)

The AdA acquired 113 Skyraiders between February 1960 and March 1962. After the end of Algerian War, they served with the EAA.21 in the Afars and Issas and Madagascar, and later with EAA.22 in Chad. These three AD-4Ns of EAA.1/21 were photographed at Fort Lamy in 1970, while fully loaded with T.10 unguided rockets and 125kg SAMP bombs. (Albert Grandolini Collection)

Skyraiders were operated under quite primitive conditions in Chad, which in turn caused a number of accidents. Without better ground equipment, all refuelling and re-arming operations necessitated plenty of back-breaking work by ground crews. (Albert Grandolini Collection)

of indigenous design.

Nevertheless, Africa remained an area of interest, primarily because of local energy resources (like oil in Gabon). Therefore, the French continued maintaining a number of bases in their former colonies in West and East Africa, most important of which were in the former territory of the Afars and the Issas (nowadays Djibouti), in Bangui, capital of the Central African Republic (CAR), but also in Chad and Cameroon. Correspondingly, and contrary to other contemporary European military powers, the French military retained an expeditionary capability, although this did not receive a priority. The army was ordered to maintain its 11th Airborne Division (Division de Parachutiste), the navy to maintain a force of two aircraft carriers, and the air force whatever assets it could spare, for possible contingencies in Africa. Each of these branches had to set up an 'intervention cell' ('Guépard Cell'), i.e. keep at least one battalion, warship or squadron respectively, on alert and ready to be deployed at 48 hours' notice.

The Armée de l'Air initially wanted to maintain a squadron of Douglas B-26 Invader light bombers for this purpose. However, budgetary constraints dictated retention of two small light squadrons equipped with Douglas AD-4N Skyraiders in Africa instead, based in Djibouti and on Madagascar. The aircraft in question were quite old and worn out by that time, and they suffered heavily when operated under 'field' conditions. Therefore, although each squadron should

have had a nominal strength of twelve aircraft, neither ever operated more than seven AD-4Ns at once.

More were not considered necessary as crisis planning envisaged their reinforcement through additional fighter-bombers deployed directly from France, the so-called 'Rapace Cell'. Understanding that any such deployments would be greatly hampered by the limited range of the aircraft involved, Paris maintained agreements for overflight rights with a number of African countries, including Algeria, Mauritania, Cote d'Ivoire, Niger, Cameroon and Gabon. During the late 1960s, the Rapace Cell was primarily drawn from AdA units operating North American F-100D Super Sabres, usually supported by some of 12 C-135F tankers/transports operated by the Air Refuelling Squadron 90 (Escadron de Ravitaillement en Vol, ERV), which was re-designated as the ERV.93 in 1976. By 1978, Super Sabres were replaced by SEPECAT Jaguar A fighter-bombers, designed to operate from short runways and capable of in-flight refuelling. Correspondingly, one squadron of the Fighter Bomber Wing 11 (Escadron de Chasse, EC), the EC.3/11 'Corse', based at Toul/Rosières AB, was trained for overseas deployments. The EC.4/11 'Jura' was trained for the same purpose by 1981, and later on all Jaguar units of the AdA were prepared for such eventualities.

Escalation to Limousin

Chad has no railroads and a 'road' network of about 33,500 kilometres, only a few of which are paved and only about one quarter

The sole SE.3180 Alouette II of the GMT raising a cloud of dust while taking off. Clouds of dust caused by the rotor downwash made nearly every take-off and landing in Chad a very risky affair. This helicopter wore only the serial 001 applied in white on lower fuselage. (Albert Grandolini Collection)

Prototype C.160 Transall as seen while unloading supplies for forward-deployed French troops, in October 1969. (Albert Grandolini Collection)

of which can be described as 'all weather' roads. Unsurprisingly, a large number of small airports were constructed under French colonial rule. Over time, no less than 55 airports, airfields and dirt strips emerged all over the country, of which only the airport at Fort Lamy was capable of accommodating large jets in the 1960s. Nevertheless, they proved crucial for deployment of French troops in the country.

The first element of the French military to deploy to Chad were eight Douglas AD-4N Skyraiders (including serials 33, 48, 49, 59 and 68) of the Light Air Support Squadron 1/21 (Escadrille d'Appui Aérien, EAA), which arrived in Fort Lamy after long flights from Djibouti and Madagascar on 30 August 1968. The fighter-bombers, which were subsequently re-deployed to Faya Largeau, were under the command of Commandante (Cdte) Blanc, and accompanied by one transport aircraft that brought in technicians, support equipment, and weapons.

Supported by AdA Skyraiders, the Chadian paras quickly brought the situation in Aouzou under control, and were withdrawn by 16 January 1969. The Skyraiders returned to Fort Lamy three days later, and then continued to Gabon, where one of them (serial 49) crashed into the sea during a training mission, killing its pilot, Lieutenant (Lt) Delcambre, on 2 February. Subsequently, the EAA.1/21 was reinforced through a detachment from EAA.2/21, and reorganised as the Light Air Support Squadron 1/22 'Ain' (Escadrille Légère d'Appui Aérien, ELAA), under the command of Capt Perret.

Deployment of the Skyraiders proved insufficient and in the following months the government lost control over most of the BET and remained only in possession of Faya Largeau, Fada, Bardai and Ouianga Kebir. Therefore, Tombalbaye was left without a choice but to request direct and more comprehensive assistance from the French government.

Concluding that the insurgents were meanwhile receiving significant support from several neighbouring countries, this time Paris launched 'Operation Limousin' and deployed no less than 1,600 troops to the country, starting on 14 April 1969. The first to arrive were 400 paras of the 2nd Parachute Regiment of the Foreign Legion (Régiment Etranger Parachutistes, REP), followed by elements of the 6th Overseas Interarms Regiment (Regiment Interarmes d'Outre-Mer, RIAOM) that arrived from their base in Gabon.[34] One month later, the ELAA.1/22 was reinforced by two AdA AD-4Ns (serials 53 and 63), while the French Army Aviation

(Aviation Légère de l'Armée de Terre, ALAT), added two Sikorsky H-34 helicopters, one of which was a so-called 'Pirate', a variant armed with a 20mm cannon installed inside the cabin.

While the ground troops managed to support the ANT and helped stabilise the situation in the BET, their aerial support apparently saw no combat operations. It is only known that Skyraider serial number 43 was written off following a takeoff accident at Fort Lamy, from which Capt Bertrand, the new commander of the ELAA.1/22, emerged unharmed on 14 June 1969.

Because of this loss and because the duration of Operation Limousin was extended in order to enable the Chadian military to destroy the insurgency, the AdA units in the country were subsequently significantly reinforced. In addition to the arrival of at least three AD-4Ns, a full squadron of Nord 2501 Noratlas transports, a mixed squadron of H-34 Cargo and H-34 Pirate helicopters (later reinforced through addition of one or two Aerospatiale SE.3180 Alouette II), one Broussard light transport and, starting in September 1969, one of C.160 Transall prototypes were deployed to Fort Lamy. As of 1 July 1969 these assets were re-organised as the Mixed Transport Group (Groupe Mixte de Transport, GMT).

Simultaneously, French and Chadian ground forces were significantly reorganised and a joint command structure introduced, with the commander of the French troops in Chad, Gen Cortadellas, in charge. Cortadellas divided the country into five Tactical Field Headquarters (Etat Majors Tactiques, EMT): EMT1 in the Mongo area, primarily held by the REP paras; EMT2 in Fort Archambault, held by the REP; EMT3 in Faya Largeau, held by ANT troops; EMT4 in Abéche, and EMT5 in N'Djamena, held by the 6th RIAOM.

Gaddafi's Pressure

A series of dramatic external events were to prove influential in the fate of Chad during the following weeks. The coup in Libya on 1 September 1969 resulted in the disbandment of King Idris II's bodyguard, and a large number of well-trained Toubous returned to Chad together with their weapons. Nearly all of them instantly joined the FROLINAT, significantly boasting its combat effectiveness. Subsequently, Gaddafi began exercising pressure upon Tombalbaye in his search for expansion of Libyan influence.

On 1 October 1969, another Skyraider (serial 59) was written off after a takeoff accident at Fort Lamy, but once again the pilot, Lt Pastorelli, came out unharmed. The remaining three examples (serials 38, 53 and 68) were re-deployed to Faya Largeau, where their crews had to work under rather 'rudimentary' conditions. For example, all the aircraft had to be refuelled with the help of hand pumps from tanks holding 2,500 litres. This flight was reinforced through the addition of a single Noratlas (serial 15) equipped to act as a 'gunship' and armed with two 20mm cannons for this purpose

---

34 The RIAOM was a famed old colonial infantry regiment, well accustomed to Chad, and was a miniature army itself, consisting of paratroopers, infantry, artillery, a company of Ferret armoured cars and an ALAT detachment with three to five Piper PA.22 Tri-Pacer light aircraft.

Rocket-armed AD-4N making a low pass over northern Chad. Although French pilots developed into true experts in operating their aircraft and helicopters at altitudes below 30 metres (90ft), this exposed them to ground fire, and the aircraft regularly returned to base full of bullet-holes as well as holes caused by splinters from detonations of their own weapons. (Albert Grandolini Collection)

Noratlas transport dropping paratroopers of the 6th CPIMa near the Central African Republic border in 1969. Except for hauling troops and supplies all over the country, one Noratlas was equipped with two 20mm cannons to serve as a gunship, while two others were equipped to drop flare bombs to light up the battlefield by night. (Albert Grandolini Collection)

Crewman Bernard Lart with a H-34 Pirate helicopter – note the 20mm cannon – in 1972. (Bernard Lart via Arnaud Delalande)

A Piper PA.22 of the ALAT as seen in Chad in 1970. (Gerard Sanz Collection)

(one of these was firing through the rear cargo doors), which also operated form Mongo and Abéche. Despite all the possible problems, these four aircraft flew a total of thirteen fire-support operations between November 1969 and October 1970, primarily in areas around Faya Largeau, Abéche, Am-Timan and Bardai.

On 19 March 1970, Gen Cortadellas launched 'Operation Ephémère', ordering a motorised element of the 2nd REP to advance from Faya Largeau towards Ounianga Kebir, where a group of around 140 insurgents was besieging the ANT garrison. A severe sandstorm forced the column to stop at Wadi Doum for a day, but the Legionnaires subsequently continued their advance. Although the same storm also grounded the AdA, they reached Ounianga Kebir on 23 March and immediately became involved in an intensive fire fight. Meanwhile, Cortadellas deployed additional paras of the 6th Marine Infantry Parachute Company (Compagnie Parachutiste d'Infanterie de Marine, CPIMa) into the area too, and these were deployed with the help of Noratlas transports and by trucks on 24 March.[35] This unit assaulted the insurgent base with close support

from Skyraiders on the following day, causing heavy losses to their opponents. As the surviving insurgents withdrew to the north of Ounianga Serir they came under repeated attacks and were finally assaulted and largely destroyed by marine commandos with support from AD-4Ns and H-34 Pirate helicopters on 27 March. In the course of these clashes, the French suffered a loss of five killed in action (KIA) and nine wounded in action (WIA), but the insurgents were decimated, losing 84 KIA and 28 captured, together with 63 weapons. Ounianga Kebir remained under ANT control.

On 29 July 1970, around 200 insurgents attacked the village of Akber Djobo, some 80km outside Abéche. During the following evening, 22 soldiers of the 4th Commando CPIMa were embarked on two Noratlases and flown to Abéche, where three H-34s were waiting from them. The helicopters then deployed the commandos about one kilometre from insurgent positions, still by night, thus starting 'Operation Moquette'. Early in the morning, the troops continued their advance supported by a Piper PA.22 Trip-Pacer, which tracked the insurgents as they ran away and scattered in the desert. The largest group of Chadians then turned around and counterattacked the commandos, forcing them to retreat under cover from two Skyraiders and one H-34 Pirate. Nevertheless,

35 There is no 'Marine Corps' as such in France, but the term 'Infanterie de Marine' is used for units trained for amphibious operations, most of which trace their traditions to former colonial units. Their soldiers are considered elite and known as 'Marsouins'.

A DC-8 SARIGUE in its original configuration, as operated over Chad in the mid-1970s. (Albert Grandolini Collection)

when the French returned to the scene of this clash a day later, they found the bodies of nineteen dead insurgents.

Later in the summer, the French contingent in Chad launched two additional counterinsurgency (COIN) operations, 'Lévrier' and 'Griffon', but the AD-4Ns deployed to support them suffered a spate of accidents, primarily caused by the harsh elements and the basic conditions under which they were operating. Serial number 26 made a belly landing at Fort Lamy, on 26 August; serial number 79, flown by Lt Barando, suffered engine failure while taking off from Fada on 3 September; and serial number 85 made an emergency landing at Zouar five days later. Correspondingly, the ELAA.1/22 was forced to send three additional aircraft to the country (serials 50, 56 and 61), and establish a permanent presence at Faya Largeau in November 1970.

Meanwhile, during October of the same year, Gen Cortadellas ordered the 6th CPIMa to scout the palm grove, extending some 50 to 120km north-west of Faya. On 11th of that month, the unit was underway from Bedo towards Kirdini when it ran into an ambush, suffering twelve KIA and 25 WIA. Survivors established contact with their base in Faya only after nightfall, requesting the emergency evacuation of casualties. An Alouette II (serial 001) from Helicopter Squadron 3/67 'Paris' (Escadrille de Hélicoptères, EH), flown by Lt Bernard Koszela and Capt Néfiolov (CO of the ELAA.1/22, who acted as navigator) was deployed for this purpose. The helicopter was supported by Noratlas serial 171 from 59 GMT, flown by Lieutenants Lalloz and Malphettes, which was dropping flare bombs. In two flights during the night, followed by two during the morning, Koszela managed to extract all the seriously injured. Two Skyraiders from ELAA.1/22, flown by WO Lourdais and CWO Corre, subsequently attempted to track down the insurgents, which suffered a loss of more than 60 KIA during this clash, but found no trace of survivors.

The 6th CPIMa hardly recovered from this blow when it was ordered to launch 'Operation Picardie II', which envisaged support for ANT units withdrawing from Mourso and Gabroa. The Chadians were evacuated during the evening of 21 October, bringing with them several captured insurgents, who provided details about a fuel base at Goubone, some 70km north-east of Zouar. On the following day this place was attacked by three H-34 Pirates and AD-4Ns armed with 125kg bombs and unguided rockets, and then mopped up by paratroopers and legionaries.

On 22 December, the French Naval Aviation (Aéronavale) deployed to Chad for the first time, initially sending several Sikorsky HSS-1 helicopters (naval variant of the S-58) from 33F Squadron to Mayounga. Amongst others, this unit became involved in 'Operation Bison' which ran between 21 and 23 January 1971 in the Borkou area, some 70km northwest of Gouro, against a group of 50 insurgents. This operation began with nine HSS-1s and one Alouette II re-deploying from Faya to Gouro, where they were refuelled from two Transalls that also brought in the commandos of the 6th CPIMa, and two sections of the 3rd Marine Infantry Regiment (Régiment d'Infanterie de Marine, RIMa). The troops then embarked on the helicopters and were flown in the direction of a reported enemy position, intending to make a landing some 1,200 metres away. Shortly afterwards, a major insurgent position was detected in a different position but the necessary information did not reach all the involved units and therefore some of helicopters flew straight into an ambush. Despite support from at least one H-34 Pirate, the commandos came under heavy fire and one of them, the son of Gen Cortadellas, was killed shortly after landing. The Pirate was hit as well; the crew managed to climb to 800m before the aircraft lost power and the pilot was forced to land with the help of autorotation. Two AD-4Ns, flown by Lieutenants Fiquemot and Michel Lourdais, which circled about 30km further south, were called to provide support and they unleashed unguided rockets and 20mm cannon fire upon the insurgents, who were subsequently encircled and put under intense pressure. When Fiquemot and Lourdais returned to Faya to refuel and re-arm, they were reinforced by a third AD-4N, flown by Cdte Pourchet. The insurgents managed to hold their position and during the following night the French troops attempted to keep them encircled. However, the Noratlas loaded with flare bombs necessary to lighten the battlefield, arrived too late, thus the Chadians managed to escape into the darkness, leaving about a dozen KIA behind them. The damaged H-34 was repaired in the field and flown back to Gouro the next morning.

The 33F was subsequently involved in operations from Bardai, where one of its helicopters (serial 454) crashed on 21 February 1971, though without consequences for the crew. Eventually, the naval helicopters were withdrawn from Chad via Fort Lamy, and were back on board the French Navy aircraft carrier *Foch* by 23 March.

The remaining French units were back in action on 7 June 1971, when the 6th CPIMa was again re-deployed from Fort Lamy to Faya Largeau in an attempt to track down a group of insurgents that had committed several atrocities against the local population. Having no vehicles, the commandos requisitioned several trucks from Libyan

Originally deployed in Afars and Issas ('French Somalia') with the EAA.1/21, AdA's AD-4N Skyraiders were moved to Chad in August 1968. Reorganised as the ELAA.1/22, this detachment introduced the insignia and markings as seen here. Primary weapons consisted of T.10 unguided rockets, 50–250kg bombs, and four 20mm cannons installed in the wings.

Six overhauled ex-AdA AD-4Ns were provided to the ENT in April 1976. Flown by French pilots, they represented the only combat element of the nascent Chadian Air Force. Outwardly, these aircraft retained much of their original livery, including the aluminium-silver colour, but with the Chadian roundel and tricolore on the rudder.

The Mirage 5D was the principal LAAF fighter-bomber during the 1970s and was sometimes deployed for interception purposes too. Except for service in Egypt during the October 1973 Arab–Israeli War, it saw action during the short Egypt–Libya War of 1977 and subsequently in Chad. The Libyans acquired this type together with a wide range of French-made weapons, including (from left to right): JL-100 combined rocket pod and drop tank, SAMP.200 bombs (installed on drop tank), Matra Type 116 and F4 rocket pods.

Rarely seen in public before 2009, the LAAF's MiG-21-fleet was primarily used for advanced training purposes during the 1970s and 1980s, especially for foreign pilots trained in Libya, such as Palestinians and Ugandans. This example was one of about two dozen overhauled by the Zmaj Works in the former Yugoslavia in the early 1980s, where it received an unusual camouflage pattern of light earth and dark olive green on top surfaces and sides, with light admiralty grey on lower surfaces. Serials were often applied in Arabic digits on the starboard (right-hand) side of the aircraft.

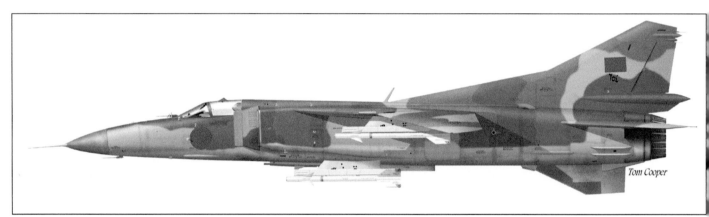

LAAF MiG-23MS serial number 654 of Benina-based No. 1040 Squadron in 1981, when this unit was entirely staffed by SyAAF personnel. Of interest is the standardised camouflage pattern for all MiG-23s exported around this time: sand (FS13523), dark earth (FS20095) and green (FS30098) on upper surfaces, with light blue-grey (FS35622) on undersurfaces.

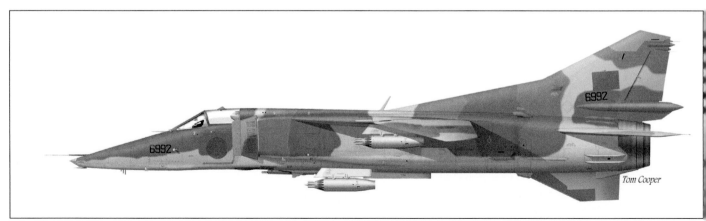

This MiG-23BN was operated by al-Abraq-based No. 1070 squadron from 1976 until 2003 (it was found abandoned at this base in March 2011). Like all other MiG-23s delivered to Libya in the 1970s and 1980s, it was painted along the same standardised camouflage pattern, and received a four-digit serial number in black on the front fuselage and the fin. It is shown armed with UV-16-57 rocket pods for sixteen 57mm rockets.

MiG-25P serial number 2204 was one of early examples of this variant operational with the LAAF. It is shown armed with one R-40RD (AA-6 Acrid) medium range air-to-air missile. All Libyan MiG-25s were painted in a colour equivalent to grey (FS36173) on upper surfaces and sides, and light grey (FS36495) on undersurfaces, though the paint on top surfaces and sides was nearly always bleached by sun and sand to a shade resembling light ghost grey (FS36375).

A MiG-25R of No. 1035 Squadron, as sighted by US Navy pilots on 18 August 1981, including the unit designation stencil on the front fuselage. Notable is that the leading edges of both wings, fins and intake insides were left in natural metal. The same was the case with the bottom of the rear fuselage (around both engines), although the colour there tended to get darker because of heat effects.

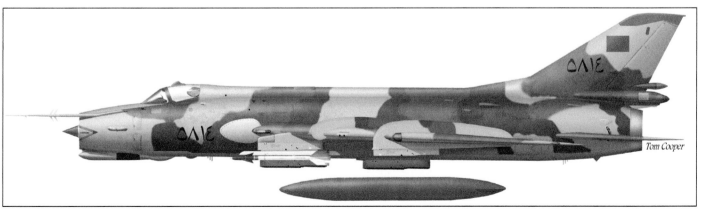

A Su-22 (without suffix) serial number 5814, as intercepted by USN pilots on 18 August 1981. The appearance of this fighter-bomber in the role of 'interceptor' caused some surprise in the West, resulting in guessing that the pilot that fired at Fast Eagle 107, on the morning of 19 August, might have done so inadvertently. However, intercepts of radio traffic removed any doubts about Libyan intentions.

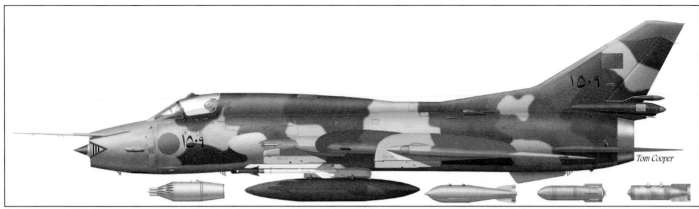

A Su-22M (or Su-22M-2K) of the LAAF No. 1032 or No. 1036 Squadron, as encountered by USN fliers on 18 April 1981. The original camouflage pattern of yellow sand and olive green was 'enhanced' through the addition of large splotches of dark olive green. Serial number 1509 was applied by hand on the front fuselage, and repeated on the fin.

A reconstruction of the 'Fast Eagle 107' – the F-14A Block 95, BuAerNo 160390 – as flown by Muczynski and Anderson on the morning of 19 August 1981, based on contemporary photographs and recollections of the pilot. Notable is the absence of AIM-54 Phoenix missiles. Because of a very strict set of ROEs, these were very seldom carried by Tomcats during operations off the Libyan coast in the 1980s.

A reconstruction of the F-14A BuAerNo 160414 (modex AJ201), assigned to the CO VF-84, Edward 'Hunyack' Andrews, during the *Nimitz's* cruise in the Mediterranean of 1981. When Andrews was attempting to engage and shoot down one of the Libyan MiG-25s on the morning of 19 August of that year, this Tomcat was armed with AIM-54 Phoenix long-range air-to-air missiles.

A Jaguar A of the EC.1/11 'Roussillon' as deployed to Chad with EC.3/11 'Corse' during Operation Tacaud. At that time Jaguars were usually armed with 125kg SAMP bombs or LAU-3 rocket pods for unguided 68mm rockets and 30mm DEFA cannons, installed internally. During the fighting for Ati, they were usually limited to making strafing runs in order to avoid causing damage to their own troops.

The LAAF began deploying Mirage F.1s inside Chad in 1981, and by 1983 they were regularly appearing in the skies over that country. The F.1ADs and F.1EDs were primarily used for ground attack, although the latter was designed as an interceptor and could be armed with Matra 530F-1 medium-range air-to-air missiles. Because of the unsuitability of the runways at Faya Largeau and elsewhere, Libyan jets could be deployed only from Aouzou during that time, which might have been the reason for their inability to intercept many French aircraft flying north of the 'Red Line' during the period 1983–1985.

A reconstruction of the LAAF Mi-25 serial number 103, shot down outside N'Djamena in December 1981. Libya received a mix of Mi-24As and Mi-25s in the late 1970s, of which the former are said to have been painted in grey and dark green, while the latter received the same camouflage pattern as Mi-25s exported to Iraq and Syria around the same time. This consisted of sand yellow and light green on upper surfaces and sides, and light admiralty grey (BS381C/697) on bottom surfaces. The inset is showing 9M17P Falanga (ASCC code 'AT-2 Swatter') ATGMs and their launch rail, and a UV-32-57 pod for unguided rockets, as usually carried by Libyan Mi-25s.

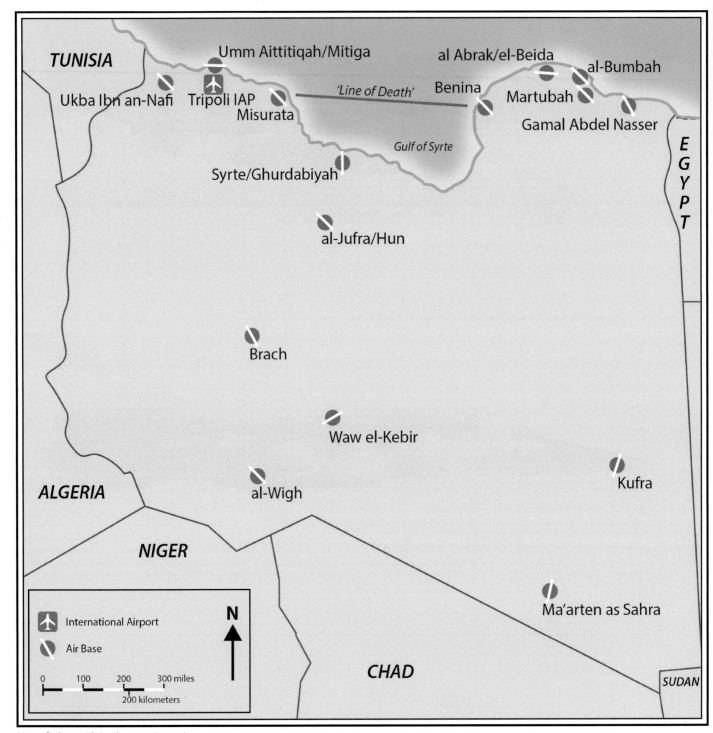

Map of Libya with its three major regions.

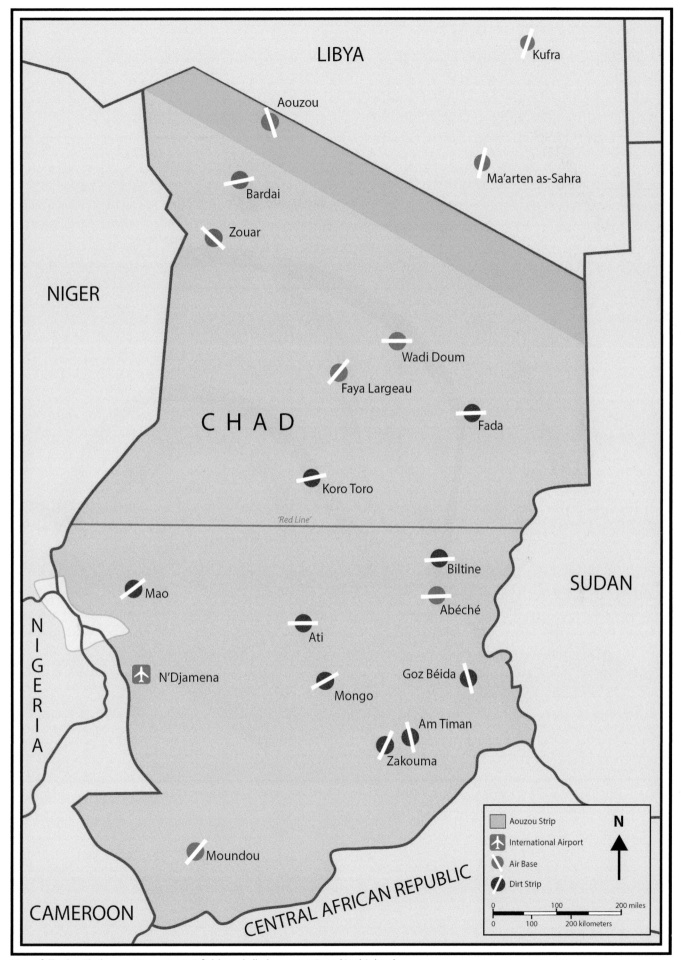

Map of Chad, with the most important airfields and all places mentioned in this book.

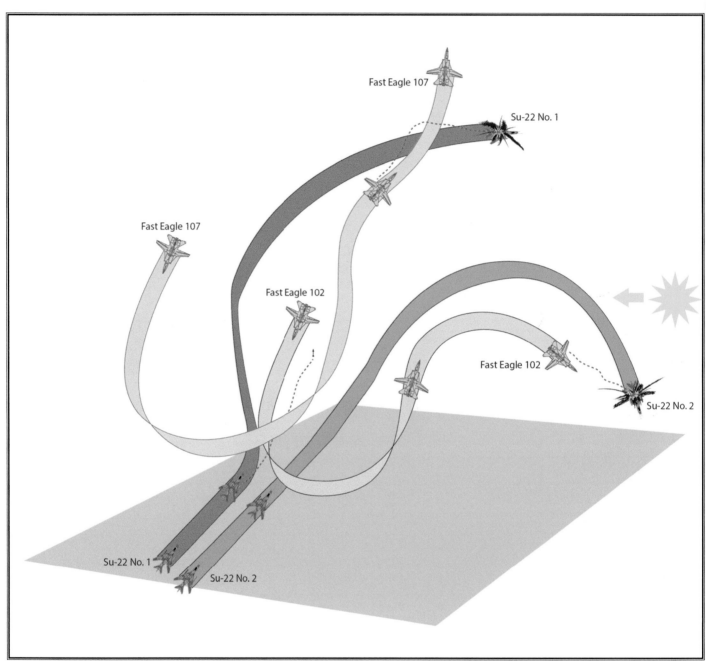

Engagement on 19 August 1980 between two F-14As, call-signs Fast Eagle 102 and Fast Eagle 107 versus two LAAF Su-22s.

Al-Husumi at the controls of one of three T-33As donated to Libya, used for training RLAF pilots at Wheelus AB. (al-Husumi Collection)

The first Mirage 5DE interceptor manufactured for Libya, as seen prior to delivery in July 1970. (Photo by Stephane Mellec)

One of the earliest orders placed by the new government in Tripoli was for sixteen C-130H Hercules. Only eight of these transports were delivered, starting in early 1971, while the remainder was subsequently embargoed and stored at Lockheed's facility in Georgia. (Photo by Mangion)

Rare photograph of one of ten Mirage 5DRs (serial number 306) acquired by Libya. Two of these were lent to No. 69 Squadron EAD and saw some service during the October 1973 Arab–Israeli War. This example was photographed at Dassault's Toulouse Plant in 1983: it was subsequently embargoed and apparently never re-delivered to Libya again. (Albert Grandolini Collection)

Twenty Boeing CH-47C Chinook helicopters, manufactured under licence by Meridionali of Italy, were ordered by Libya in the mid-1970s. Delivered from 1979 onwards, they saw extensive service during the subsequent war in Chad, while almost exclusively being flown and serviced by contracted US and British personnel. (Martin Hornliman/Milpix Collection)

According to recollections of former Yugoslav Air Force instructors that used to work in Libya during the mid-1970s, Soviet-operated Libyan SAMs, primarily SA-6s that can be seen in this photograph from 1976, should have caused significant losses to the Egyptian Air Force. (Gaddafi Collection)

Troops of the 2nd REP taking a break during a patrol in northern Chad in late 1960s. (Albert Grandolini Collection)

This rare colour photograph of the AD-4N operated by the ELAA.1/22 reveals that the fin and wing tips, as well as wheel bay covers, were painted in blue. Notable is the absence of national markings on the bottom wing surfaces. (S. P. via Arnaud Delalande)

A H-34 Pirate of the 59th GMT at Faya Largeau airfield in 1970. GMT's helicopters were usually marked only with two-letter codes, the first of which was 'H'. Except for 'HD' seen here, other known Pirates were HC and HR. (via Albert Grandolini)

A H-34 Cargo of the GMT, coded SKY819/HT. (via Albert Grandolini)

An AD-4N overflying two Noratlas transports at Fada airfield in 1972. (Bernard Lart via Arnaud Delalande)

An AD-4N operated by the ENT seen while moving out for a training sortie in the mid-1970s. Except for national insignia, and their BuAerNo (usually stencilled on the fin root), they seem not to have received any other kind of markings. (Albert Grandolini Collection)

Three ENT AD-4Ns as seen at N'Djamena IAP. The aircraft in the centre was serialled 125880. All were flown by French pilots. (Albert Grandolini Collection)

French withdrawal from Chad in 1979 sealed the fate of the ENT, the aircraft of which were left to rot around different corners of N'Djamena IAP. This photograph from 1986 shows one of three ENT Reims-Cessna FTB.337s delivered in 1977, with a Socata Rallye 235 registered as TT-MAE in the background. (Albert Grandolini Collection)

Constructed in the late 1950s, the USS *Forrestal* (*CV-59*) was the first of USN's 'super carriers', but still a very powerful ship equipped with the most advanced electronics available in 1981. (USN)

Nuclear powered USS *Nimitz* (*CVN-68*) was the newest and most modern aircraft carrier with the US Navy in 1981. Contrary to the CVW-17 embarked on board USS *Forrestal*, the *Nimitz's* CVW-8 also included two squadrons equipped with F-14 Tomcats, then the most advanced fighter-interceptors in world-wide service. (USN)

Unusually for the 1980s, the CVW-8 included the EA-6B Prowler electronic countermeasures aircraft of the VMAQ-2 Playboy Squadron of the US Marine Corps. Although little was publicly reported, with the help of intelligence provided by Tolkachev, the aircraft proved highly effective in jamming Libyan ground-based radars, and radars of LAAF interceptors during most of encounters on 18 and 19 August 1981. (USN)

A scene from Cairo West AB during the Bright Star '81 multinational exercise, showing USAF E-3s, B-52s and C-130s, together with their crews and support personnel. (USAF)

Self-protrait of a VF-84-crew. The colourful F-14As of this squadron, adorned by its traditional 'skull and crossbones' insignia, became famous in the 1980s. (USN)

Although the AdA and the LAAF flew a number of patrols along the Red Line, and although the Libyans maintained a well-developed radar network in northern Chad, the pilots from the two air forces seldom met in the air. Even LAAF Mirage F.1EDs that were deployed at Aouzou between 1983–1985 never managed to intercept any of the many French reconnaissance aircraft that repeatedly returned over the area even after the French withdrawal. (Claudio Tosselli Collection)

The plan for Operation Early Call envisaged enticing the LAAF to send its aircraft over Sudan, where they would be intercepted by Egyptian and Sudanese fighters, supported by USAF and US Navy aircraft. Here a F-4E Phantom II of the Egyptian Air Force (armed with AIM-9B Sidewinder missiles) is about to take fuel from a KC-10A Extender tanker of the US Air Force. (USAF)

A Jaguar A (coded A118/11-YF) from EC.11 seen while being bombed up prior to a sortie from N'Djamena IAP, during the early stages of Operation Manta in 1983. (Albert Grandolini Collection)

civilians, loaded them with supplies and fuel for the helicopters and then drove all the way to Bedo, where they were joined by four H-34 Cargos, one H-34 Pirate, and a single Alouette II. When the insurgents were detected while camping at Kouroudi, some 40km further north, it turned out there were around 150 of them. Despite the enemy's numerical superiority, the French decided to attack and did so during the afternoon of 9 June, with full support from H-34s and two Skyraiders from Faya. Achieving complete surprise, the commandos assaulted as planned, encircling the insurgents, killing 55 and seriously injuring 35, in exchange for two fatalities. However, the sun then went down and once again the Noratlas equipped with flare bombs arrived too late, letting the surviving Chadians make good their escape into the night.

Loss of Aouzou Strip

The French military presence and the successful COIN operations in the BET proved insufficient. On 17 September 1971, Libya officially recognised the FROLINAT and started supporting it with money, arms (including more than 100 modern automatic assault rifles), ammunition and supplies smuggled over the border. Tombalbaye's government attempted to make a number of concessions, including political reforms, abolition of many of the new taxes and reinstatement of local leaders in Sahelian prefectures, but to no avail. On the contrary, the French decision to withdraw all troops from the BET by the end of 1971 only encouraged Gaddafi to reinforce his support for the insurgents and subversion within the ANT. After the later staged an abortive coup attempt, in April 1971, Tombalbaye's government broke diplomatic relations to Libya, but this only resulted in Tripoli reinforcing its pressure.

In 1972, Libyan police and gendarmes occupied the contested Aouzou Strip, Gaddafi justifying his claims by by citing the Vichy–Italian treaty. Subsequently, the Libyan Army units deployed in the area as well, followed by the first LAAF units, which arrived as soon as a new runway was constructed in Aouzou.

Under pressure, Tombalbaye was forced to make additional concessions. While admitting that his government had lost control of the BET, he broke relations with Israel and re-established diplomatic ties to Tripoli. Furthermore, and partially following developments in the Democratic Republic of the Congo (or Congo-Kinshasa), subsequently renamed to Zaire, he 'Africanised' the country. The most significant change introduced during this period was the replacement of French and European names with indigenous names. Amongst others, Fort Lamy was re-named as N'Djamena, and Tombalbaye changed his first name from Francois to N'Garta. His other decisions took the country in a new, disastrous, direction. Tombalbaye abandoned most political and economic reforms and began purging the top officers of the ANT, accusing them of 'political sorcery', and replacing them with his favourites. Any non-Christian or non-Muslim candidates for public and military service were required to undergo initiations into the Sara yondo rites. Pleased by this development, and Tombalbaye's critique of French politics in Africa, Gaddafi restricted support for the FROLINAT, enabling the ANT, supported by French advisers, to successfully confine the Second Liberation Army to remote corners of the BET.

It was under these unusual circumstances that the French launched 'Operation Languedoc', aimed at destroying the core of the Third Liberation Army FROLINAT, totalling around 320 fighters active in eastern Chad, in early 1972. On 12 February, the 6th CPIMa, commanded by Lt Col Tonquedec, and the ANT, launched a large-scale search for a convoy of weapons that was expected to arrive from Sudan. This was located some three kilometres south-

east of the village of Am Dagachi. Six days later it was attacked by commandos, supported by one H-34 Pirate and several H-34 Cargos. The insurgents fought back with vigour, damaging one Cargo and forcing the Pirate to make an emergency landing. The PA.22 that was tracking insurgents was either hit by ground fire and shot down, or crashed due to flying too low, killing the pilot WO Dartigaux, CPIMa battalion commander Cdte Le Puloch and Lt Laval-Gilly who was in charge of the ALAT detachment in Mongo. Following the arrival of reinforcements, the French stormed the convoy, killing 49 insurgents and capturing seven, together with a cache of 69 different weapons.

Tombalbaye's End

Languedoc was the last significant French operation in Chad of that period. Subsequently, Tombalbaye requested the French to withdraw their forces from the country, and Paris agreed to do so. The French contingent in Chad was officially disbanded and the last troops left by 28 August 1972, although a detachment remained in N'Djamena in order to continue providing military technical assistance. Included in this detachment was a small number of AD-4N Skyraiders from EAA.1/22, based at Abéche, together with several ALAT helicopters and light aircraft.[36]

In the course of Operation Limousin, the French suffered 39 KIA and 102 WIA, while the ANT is known to have suffered more than 200 fatalities. Certainly, various FROLINAT factions lost many more fighters. However, they were anything but eliminated, although the government managed to restore its authority over much of the BET and eastern Chad.

During the closing stages of their presence, the French also flew two reconnaissance missions in support of a search for several European hostages held by the FROLINAT. On 11 September 1974, a formation consisting of a Mirage IVA serial 54 (flown by Commandants Lannevere and Jeantet) and five Boeing C-135F tankers, crossed the Mediterranean and then entered either Algeria or Egypt and Sudan to reach Chad. The Mirage IV separated to make its photo run over designated targets, before rejoining the formation to return to Bordeaux. Only three days later the AdA launched 'Operation Rebelote', this time deploying a single Douglas DC-8 Sarrique ELINT/SIGINT reconnaissance aircraft to search for possible electronic emissions from the target area, which the Mirage IV might have missed. The success of both of these sorties, and Paris paying the ransom for its citizens, were in vain. Cdre Galopin, who acted as a mediator with the FROLINAT, was executed on the order from Oueddei, on 4 April 1975. Another hostage managed to escape in May 1975, while the last two were released only in January 1977.

In the meantime, Tombalbaye began fiercely criticising leading ANT commanders for their poor performance in operations against the insurgents. Continuous arrests eventually prompted junior officers to stage a mutiny and order the gendarmerie units in N'Djamena to overthrow and kill the president on 13 April 1974. Toimbalbaye was succeeded by General Felix Malloum, freshly released from prison, who instantly reaffirmed his cooperation with the French.

In an attempt to improve the position of his weak government, Malloum enlisted the First Liberation Army FROLINAT, led by Ahmed Acyl and primarily including Chadian Arabs, to counter the threat from the Libyan-backed Second Liberation Army, which largely consisted of Toubou tribesmen and was led by Goukouni

---

36 According to log-books of involved AdA pilots, Skyraiders based in Abéche averaged some 35 operational sorties a month between July 1972 and June 1975, when they were finally withdrawn.

Oueddei and Hissène Habré. This measure was overtaken by subsequent developments. Oueddei and Habré split over personal differences (primarily related to the question of Libyan support), with the vehemently anti-Libyan Habré creating a new faction. Combined with their poor supply situation and the subsequent

drought, this eventually resulted in infighting between the insurgents and then an outright civil war, which in turn prompted direct Libyan military intervention in Chad, bringing the country to ruin.[37]

37 Turner, pp. 169–170.

CHAPTER 4
EARLY LIBYAN INTERVENTIONS

Through the mid-1970s, Libya continued providing military and technical assistance to Oueddei's Second Liberation Army to such an extent that this organisation was re-organised as the Popular Armed Forces (Forces Armées Populaires, FAP). The FAP was actually a conventional military force consisting of around 2,000 truck-mounted light infantry and a company of about 100 commandos, supported by battalions of Libyan MBTs, armoured cars, artillery and the Libyan Air Force. The LAAF was meanwhile also considerably re-organised by Col Salleh Abdullah Salleh, and thus able to support the coming offensive with not only one squadron of Mirages (it remains unclear whether these were Mirage 5s or F.1s), but also a large unit equipped with SF.260 light strikers and Mi-25 helicopter gunships completely staffed by Libyans. To prove even more important was the support provided by LAAF transport aircraft and helicopters, although this area, together with maintenance, was still an issue which for the Libyans necessitated foreign support, as recalled by Hussein:

> Bolstered by our earlier experiences, during the LAAF deployment in Chad, we recruited a number of American mercenary pilots and technicians to fly and maintain our CH-47s and C-130s in that country.[38]

Malloum was not idle either, although he did not manage to re-organise and re-arm the ANT to a similar extent. Nevertheless, in April 1976 France provided six AD-4N Skyraiders and four retired AdA pilots (all recruited and paid for by Paris), and up to thirteen C-47s and Douglas C-54s, together with the necessary technicians to N'Djamena, where they formed the core of the National Chadian Squadron (Escadrille Nationale Tchadienne, ENT).

The ENT saw its first major action in late June and early July 1977, by which time it was reinforced by two AD-4Ns of the Gabonese Presidential Guard, flown by two ex-AdA pilots, Jacques Borne and René Gras. The action in question was prompted by a FROLINAT attack on Zouar and Malloum's order for the ENT to counterattack. The small force moved most of its assets to Faya Largeau, and began launching reconnaissance missions in order to obtain a

better insight into the insurgent strength, positions and activities. This included one C-47 that carried Col Jean-Louis Delayen, chief adviser to General Malloum and de facto Commander-in-Chief of the ANT. Eventually the French went into action on 1 July, initially subjecting the insurgent positions to repeated Skyraider attacks, each of which was armed with two 250kg bombs, ten T-10 rockets and four hundred 20mm shells for their cannons. The ground fire they received in response was fierce and practically every aircraft involved returned with several bullet holes in the fuselage and wings. This prompted the pilots to change their tactics and attack from an altitude of only 60 metres on the next day, releasing all of their weapons in quick succession. While this left them less exposed to ground fire, the blast from bomb and rocket detonations caused so many problems, that several aircraft were damaged by it. Indeed,

France donated a total of thirteen C-47s and C-54s to the ENT and these saw extensive service during the mid-1970s. This C-47 was photographed while flying over southern Chad. (Albert Grandolini Collection)

The ubiquitous Aermacchi SF.260WL was available in large numbers. It was deployed as a light striker and armed with pods with machine guns, unguided rockets and light bombs. It played a very important role during early stages of Libyan military involvement in Chad. (Tom Cooper Collection)

38 This enterprise was run via a number of ex-Central Intelligence Agency (CIA) operatives headed by Edwin Wilson, who had been recruiting pilots and engineers for the Libyans through an office in London. Recruited US pilots flew transport and support sorties into Chad and were particularly needed for the CH-47 helicopters and C-130 Hercules transports. The entire affair ended only in 1981, when it was revealed to the media, provoking a scandal in the USA, followed by another in Great Britain, in 1983, which erupted when it became known that British pilot John Stubbs – who used to work for Wilson – attempted to re-sell seven ex-Australian C-130s to Libya. Finally, in 1984 it became known that Wilson had not only established an airline, Jamahiriya Air Transport, but that this was primarily busy trafficking arms, ammunition and spares to and from Libya, Ethiopia and Iran.

Except for SF.260WLs, the LAAF intensively deployed its then brand new Mi-25 helicopter gunships in Chad in the period 1978–1981. Although lacking the power for 'hot and high' operations, this aircraft proved popular in service because of its ability to survive significant volumes of damage. (via Ali Tani)

Wreckage of the ENT C-54 shot down near Faya Largeau on 30 January 1978. Thanks to the skilful performance of the pilots, the crew of five survived an emergency landing in the desert. (Albert Grandolini Collection)

French Army jeep (note inscription 'Djibouti') with an AdA Transall and an ENT C-47 in the background. (Albert Grandolini Collection)

the Skyraider flown by Jacques Borne came back with two holes in the canopy, both caused by splinters from its own bombs.

The inevitable happened on 3 July, when AD-4N serial 19 was hit in the engine and René Gras was forced to make an emergency landing on a small strip outside Zouar, abandoned by the ANT but not controlled by insurgents. Gras was quickly evacuated by Borne, who landed nearby. With insurgents ignoring the abandoned Skyraider, a C-47 of the ENT flew in a team of technicians that quickly repaired the damaged aircraft, and flew it out the following morning.

Advance on N'Djamena

Despite further efforts by the ENT, Zouar was overrun by the FAP on 6 July 1977, followed by Bardai and Tibesti. Meanwhile, following extensive preparations, Gaddafi and Oueddei unleashed their next major attack in January 1978. The FAP first overran all ANT garrisons in Tibesti before joining two mechanised brigades of the Libyan Army and advancing in the direction of Faya Largeau. Their approach was supported by LAAF helicopters and transports, and nervously monitored by French pilots assigned to the ENT. On 29 January 1978, the C-47 flown by Chief WO Gilbert Legoff and Major Scabello was underway on low altitude reconnaissance in the Zouar area. Unfortunately for the crew, Legoff flew so low that his wheels touched the turret of a Libyan BTR-60 APC just as the aircraft came under intense small arms fire. Moments later, the plane was hit by an SA-7 in the wing, causing it to crash. The next day, the ENT organised a rescue operation, deploying DC-4 serial 936 with barrels of fuel and the necessary spares for one SA.330 Puma helicopter and one AD-4N to Faya Largeau. From there, the transport flew in the direction of Zouar to search for the crash zone. Only a few minutes later, barely 30 kilometres outside Faya, the aircraft came under attack from two SA-7s, each of which hit a wing. With two engines on fire, the pilot was left with no choice but to make an emergency landing in the desert. All five crew members were evacuated safely, only seconds before their load of fuel went up in a big ball of flames. By the time an ALAT Puma arrived from Faya to recover the survivors, the insurgents and Libyans were already on the scene, and the helicopter came under small arms fire. Nevertheless, the crew of the downed C-54 was evacuated safely with close support from the Skyraider.

With the ENT out of action because of the SA-7-threat, the

5,000-strong ANT garrison in Faya was left exposed to sustained air strikes by Libyan SF.260s and Mi-25s. Lacking the firepower to hit back, the garrison collapsed. The majority of the troops fled the battlefield while around 1,500 ended up as prisoners of war on 18 February 1978.[39]

The Libyans and Oueddei then re-organised their forces, leaving behind a reinforced battalion of around 800 to garrison Faya and deploying a motorised force for a swift advance in the direction of Ounianga-Kebir, Fada, and Koro-Toro. All three places were secured within the next few days, before the invaders continued in the direction of Salal and Ati, which came under attack on 18 May 1978.

Operation Tacaud

With his units smashed by enemy tanks and air power, General Malloum was left with no choice but to request help from Paris. The French agreed, and launched 'Operation Tacaud' early in April 1978. In the course of this, they deployed elements of the Foreign Legion and two companies of commandos, supported by armoured cars to N'Djamena, with additional elements of the AdA and ALAT from abroad.

The AdA and the ENT went into action during the fighting for Salal on 16 April, where the ANT's French-operated AML-90 armoured cars became involved in fighting BTR-152 APCs operated by the FROLINAT. The AMLs knocked out at least one APC, but the ENT AD-4N flown by Sgt Jean-Louis Latour was shot down by an SA-7 and the pilot was killed. Two Puma helicopters (one armed with a 20mm cannon) were sent to find the crash site and the downed pilot, but one of them was also damaged by ground fire and barely managed to return to Moussoro. Despite several fierce attacks

39 Pollack, p. 376.

A fascinating photograph taken through the periscope of one of RICM's AMLs as a column was entering the town of Foundouk on 14 December 1978. The RICM vehicles passed down the main street after assaulting its southern entrance, where one AML-90 was destroyed by an RPG-7. (Albert Grandolini Collection)

Operation Tacaud saw the first deployment of the then brand new SEPECAT Jaguar A fighter-bombers operated by EC.11 in Chad. At that time, the Jaguars were still wearing their 'Europe' camouflage pattern, in Gris Vert Foncé (dark green-grey) and Gris Bleu Trés Foncé (very dark blue-grey) on top sides, with undersides in aluminium colour.

A pair of Jaguar As together with two Noratlas transports on the tarmac of N'Djamena in April 1978. (Albert Grandolini Collection)

Rare photograph of one of ALAT's Alouette IIIs deployed to Chad during Operation Tacaud while firing an SS.11 ATGM. Notable is that the helicopter wore an unusual camouflage pattern, and was coded CXN (in black). (Albert Grandolini Collection)

An Atlantic and two Jaguars seen shortly after taking off from Dakkar International for deployment to Chad. The installation in Senegal was developed into one of the major bases for French fighter bombers in Africa, with aircraft regularly rotating in and out. Extensive maintenance was usually undertaken at Bangui's M'Poko, in the CAR. (Albert Grandolini Collection)

5th RHC.

The French were in action almost immediately. When Oueddei's insurgents and Libyans overran the important town of Ati, on 18 May, Gen Bredèche ordered a company from the 3rd RIMa, supported by sixteen AML-90s from the 1st REC into a counterattack. A reconnaissance sortie by two Jaguars the next morning revealed that the heavily armed enemy was meanwhile well entrenched inside the town. Unsurprisingly, the commandos encountered heavy resistance while approaching and suffered several casualties, including one KIA. Ati was then subjected to a series of attacks by Jaguars, after which the town was assaulted. Following this clash, the French counted 80 dead insurgents and seven destroyed vehicles. They captured a number of light artillery pieces and mortars, as well as 70 AK-47s, while suffering another KIA and five WIA.

As soon as Ati was cleared, the French attacked Acyl Ahmat's insurgent force of between 500 and 600, which had been re-organised as the Democratic Revolutionary Council (Conseil Démocratique Révolutionaire, CDR) and concentrated in the Djedda area. Following reconnaissance by Jaguars, and reinforced by armoured cars from the 1st Cavalry Regiment of the Foreign Legion (Règiment Etranger de Cavalerie, REC), the 3rd RIMa assaulted the town on 31 May and secured it in the course of a sharp clash, all the time supported by AdA fighter-bombers and the sole

by Skyraiders ordered by the new French commander in Chad, Gen Bredèche, the ANT garrison in Salal was eventually overrun by around 500 well-armed insurgents. Realising the seriousness of the situation, the government in Paris then authorised the deployment of twelve Jaguar As of EC.3/11 'Corse' from Dakar in Senegal, one Breguet Br.1150 Atlantic long-range maritime patrol and reconnaissance aircraft and two C-135F tankers from France to N'Djamena on 27 April 1978. The ALAT added five Cessna L-19Es, eight SA.330 Pumas (including two 'Pirates') and six SE.319B Alouette IIIs (including two armed with SS.11 ATGMs) from the

Crew of an SA.330 Puma helicopter with jeep-mounted Legionaires of the 2nd REP in front of a typical Chaidan 'graal' (hut) in 1978. (Albert Grandolini Collection)

An AML-60 armoured car of the 3rd RICM, as seen in Abéche area in March 1979. (Albert Grandolini Collection)

Atlantic. It was in the course of this battle that the EC.11 suffered its first ever loss in Chad, when Jaguar serial number A52, flown by Lt Col Leon Pachebat, was shot down by fire from a DShK heavy machine gun during a strafing run. With one of the engines on fire and an aircraft out of control, Pachebat was forced to eject, and was recovered some 20 minutes later by a Puma helicopter. Eventually, the French captured a cache of more than 200 weapons in Djedda, including a dozen SA-7.[40]

If the appearance of French troops in Chad did not deter Gaddafi and Oueddei from ordering their forces to continue the march on N'Djamena, the appearance of AdA's Jaguars left a lasting impression upon the LAAF. Not only that, following negative experiences from the war with Egypt, Col Sallal could not recommend that his force engage the expertly trained and highly experienced French in a battle for air superiority, but Gaddafi was also not keen to enter a war with France. Without air support, the CDR, the FAP and the Libyan troops were obviously exposed to the French air power in the barren desert, and without hope of continuing their advance on the capital, as al-Bajigni concluded:

> We got bogged down in Chad, in a big blunder. Gaddafi's original plan to conquer Chad was actually not difficult to implement. However, our commanders proved unable to realise it, because they lacked training and experience. All our efforts were in vain; our advance was stopped cold, our ground troops exposed in the open and forced to withdraw.

Defeat of Volcan Army

Another problem the Libyans faced by the summer of 1978 was caused by major differences between the CDR and the FAP. Acyl's armed force, which had been re-organised as the Volcan Army, was pro maintaining close cooperation with the Libyans, but it lacked the firepower and experience necessary to continue the war even if supported by them. Conversely, Oueddei's Toubous were experienced fighters, but never comfortable with Libyans. They considered this alliance a temporary measure necessary to help them obtain control of the country. Resulting differences culminated in a fierce battle between these two groups in Faya Largeau on 27 August 1978, and a break-down of relations between Gaddafi and Oueddei.

Fiercely anti-Libyan, Habré ably exploited this situation, and put his force of about 2,000 well-armed fighters, reorganised as

the Armed Forces of the North (Forces Armées du Nord, FAN), at Malloun's disposal, who in turn appointed him as prime minister. Patiently waiting for an opportunity, Habré then spent several months plotting his next move, before deploying the FAN around key points in N'Djamena and attacking on 11 February 1979. The ENT and French forces attempted to help Malloun, but Habré warned them that he could not guarantee the security of expatriates in the Chadian capital if the bombardment continued. Despite protests from Malloun, the French suspended further bombardment. The AdA Noratlas and Transall transports helped evacuate around 3,500 expatriates to M'Poko International Airport (IAP), and then all the French units withdrew from Chad. This withdrawal effectively sealed the fate of the ENT as well, and the small force was practically disbanded and all of its aircraft left to rot in different corners on the military side of N'Djamena International.

Amid fierce battles all over N'Djamena in which nearly 4,000 Chadians were killed, Habré's FAN defeated the ANT and ousted Malloun. Not eager to let his rival take control on his own, Oueddei meanwhile rushed about 2,000 FAN fighters all the way from Tibesti to the Chadian capital, reaching it on 23 February 1979. Avoiding a mutually costly battle, the two leaders agreed to strike a deal based, to a considerable extent, on their common desire to get the Libyans out of Chad. Mediation from the international community eventually resulted in the establishment of the Transitional National Government (Government d'Union Nationale de Transition, GUNT), led by Muhammad Choua, with Oueddei as Minister of the Interior and Habré as Minister of Defence, on 29 April 1979.

During negotiations that led to the establishment of the GUNT, a force of around 800 CDR insurgents, supported by two Libyan mechanised battalions (with around 50 T-55s and Cascavel armoured cars) attacked Abéche on 5 March 1979. The town and the nearby airfield with an asphalt runway were secured by the troops of the 3rd RIMa and armoured cars of the 1st Squadron of the Armoured Marine Infantry Regiment (Régiment d'Infanterie Chars de Marine, RICM). They were supported by the 11th Battery of the Marine Artillery Regiment (Régiment d'Artillerie de Marine, RAM), and an ALAT detachment consisting of two Pumas and two Aérospatiale SE.316B Alouette III helicopters (the latter were armed with French-made SS-11 anti-tank guided missiles (ATGMs)). The fighting quickly turned against the attackers. They were allowed to enter the town and then blocked, surrounded and exposed to murderous fire from well concealed positions. In exchange for two French commandos KIA, the CDR and Libyans suffered a loss of

---

40 Pachebat's Jaguar is sometimes cited as shot down by an SA-7, apparently because two of these Soviet-made MANPADS were fired at the Jaguar flown by his wingman.

Libyan Army T-55 tanks
during a parade in
Tripoli in the late 1970s
(notice the tool boxes
installed on the left side
of their turret which
indicate they came
from Czechoslovak
production lines).
(Gaddafi Collection)

French troops inspecting a knocked-out Libyan BTR-152 APC
(background) and bodies of two Libyan Army troops following the battle
of Abéche in April 1979. (Albert Grandolin)

Two FROLINAT jeeps and a cache of arms captured from insurgents during
the battle of Abéche. (Albert Grandolini Collection)

more than 300 dead and around 850 weapons lost (including thirteen
machine guns, twelve RPG-7 launchers, five 81mm mortars and 34
SA-7s), six jeeps with recoilless 106mm guns and 36 other vehicles
with countless boxes with ammunition and mines.

Tunisian Intermezzo

On 26 January 1980, a group of around 100 well-armed, Libyan-
trained Tunisians organised as the National Front of Progressive
Forces (Front National des Forces Progressistes, FNFP), crossed the
border into Tunis. Exploiting the preoccupation of the locally-based
12th Infantry Regiment of the Tunisian Army with an exercise, they
quickly overwhelmed the few guards and occupied the town and

oasis of Gafsa. Without success, the insurgents then attempted to
'raise' the local population against Bourguiba's government.

Although forewarned about this attack by its intelligence agency,
the Tunisian government was confused at first, but then ordered
the army to counterattack. On the morning of 27 January 1980, two
Aermacchi MB.326s of Escadrille 11 of Tunisian Air Force, forward
deployed at Djerba Airport, appeared low over Gafsa. Because they
were promised support by the LAAF, the FNFP combatants came
out to 'greet' the jets, but these then made several strafing passes and
they hit a bus full of insurgents, causing heavy losses. Actually, and
contrary to the information provided by their Libyan advisers, the
radios they received were simply too short-ranged and they could
not call for air support from Tripoli.

Tunisian Army infantry units retook Gafsa in the course of an
assault launched on 3 February 1980, supported by Austrian-made

Libyan Crotale transporter-erector-launcher vehicle, knocked out during the fighting outside N'Djamena in December 1981. (Albert Grandolini Collection)

Wreckage of the LAAF Mi-25 helicopter gunship serial '103', shot down during the battle for N'Djamena in December 1980. In the foreground lies a UV-16-32 pod for unguided rockets with several live rounds still inside. (Albert Grandolini Collection)

Libyan BTR-60 APC, knocked out during the fighting in northern Chad in 1978. (Albert Grandolini Collection)

LAAF Tu-22 saw intensive action during the Libyan advance on N'Djamena in late 1980. During this period, No. 1022 Squadron was frequently flying up to four sorties a day. Much more was neither necessary nor possible, also because the crews involved usually returned completely exhausted from lengthy missions. (USN)

SK-105 Kürassier tank-hunters of the 31st Armoured Regiment, and AML-90 armoured cars of the Light Motorised Regiment. The surviving insurgents then fell back towards the Libyan border, pursued by Tunisian helicopters and their commander, Ahmed al-Marghani, was arrested at el-Hamma.

Following this experience, Bourguiba requested help from his allies. France reacted by sending Transall transports and Puma helicopters that helped re-deploy additional units of the Tunisian Army to the border with Libya. These countered a significant concentration of the Libyan Army's mechanised units. Subsequently, the USA began providing military aid to Tunisia, including deliveries of Bell UH-1H helicopters and C-130H transports.

Gaddafi's Come-Back
The first GUNT government in Chad lasted only three months. Offended that the new administration did not include any representatives of the Volcan Army, nor had it accepted the Libyan occupation of Aouzou Strip, Gaddafi ordered a new offensive into Chad. Undertaken by several mechanised battalions grouped into two brigade commands and closely supported by the LAAF, this offensive reached Faya Largeau in April 1979. However, neither the Libyan Army, nor the Volcan insurgents were a match for the GUNT troops supported by French air power. Following three months of bitter fighting for the biggest oasis in northern Chad, the Libyans

and Volcan Army were forced to withdraw in August of the same year. During the same month, another internationally mediated agreement about the composition of the GUNT government was held in Lagos. An agreement was reached according to which Oueddei was appointed President and Habré Minister of Defence. Even this agreement did not hold for more than a few months, as the two Chadian 'revolutionaries' continued quarrelling all the time. Eventually, Habré quit the GUNT government and, supported by his loyalists, again staged an attempted coup with the FAN, in the course of which he forced most of the loyal GUNT units out of N'Djamena on 20 March 1980. Attempting to secure the rest of the country, Habré then advanced on Bokoro and Mongo, but was beaten back by local GUNT garrisons. After regrouping, he advanced on Faya Largeau instead, and subsequently secured Ounianga Kebir and the Toubou plains. Returning to N'Djamena, on 1 April 1980 the FAN defeated a GUNT force led by Col Kamougue and, in the course of a battle on the Chari River, south of the capital, in turn forced him and Oueddei to flee to Tripoli and again plead for Libyan help.

Eager to avenge earlier defeats, Gaddafi was happy to provide the GUNT survivors with bases in southern Libya, where they were rested, re-organised and re-armed. They were then put under the command of a Libyan Army officer, Col Mansour Abd al-Azziz. Ironically, because the reorganised GUNT now included Kamougue and his primarily Christian troops, whereas Habré's FAN consisted exclusively of Muslims, Gaddafi thus ended up in a paradoxical situation. However, more interested in finding a winning team than in imposing Islam in Chad, the Libyan leader then mustered a brigade of foreign fighters, including a number of forcefully recruited expatriate workers, into the 'Islamic Legion'. This was to provide fire-support for the GUNT, together with 7,000 Libyan troops and 300 armoured vehicles of the Libyan Army. In order to avoid a possible costly clash between the LAAF and the AdA, the Libyans this time deployed two air defence battalions into Chad, one including French-made Crotale and the other Soviet-made SA-6 SAMs, supported by two ZSU-23-4 (radar-controlled) self-propelled anti-aircraft guns (SPAAGs) each.

The new invasion began with Ilyushin Il-76 and C-130 transports of the LAAF airlifting GUNT-fighters and the Islamic Legion into the Aouzou Strip. They were joined by Libyan mechanised forces and then launched a rapid advance on Faya Largeau on 15 October 1980.

Habré's FAN was not yet entirely in control of the BET; he had only about 4,000 fighters under arms, no armour or artillery, or even anti-tank weapons. Starting 9 October 1980, the Libyans saturated the FAN garrison in Faya with air strikes, deploying Mi-25 helicopter gunships, SF.260s, Mirages and even Tu-22s to bomb it for nearly a week. Reportedly, their air strikes did not cause lots of physical damage. However, the Libyan bombers did leave a lasting impression upon Habré's fighters through the sheer terror of their continuous presence. Correspondingly, battle-hardened GUNT fighters experienced little problems in assaulting Faya, in early November.

For the next few weeks, the local airfield was transformed into a major supply hub, to which the LAAF airlifted immense quantities of supplies, ammunition, additional troops and equipment. After a conference with Gaddafi in Faya on 4 November, al-Azziz intensified preparations before ordering a task force under the command of Col Radwan Salleh Radwan, composed of about 4,000 GUNT fighters and nearly 100 Libyan tanks and armoured vehicles, into a major advance in direction of N'Djamena. By late November 1980, Radwan's units reached Dougia, some 60 kilometres north of Chadian capital, where another supply base was set up. Obviously, the Libyans expected fierce resistance inside N'Djamena and they

wanted to avoid a situation where they would have to haul all the necessary ammunition and supplies all the way from Faya or even from bases inside Libya. Once ready, Radwan ordered his BM-21 multiple rocket launchers and the LAAF Mi-25s and SF.260 that were deployed forward at Dougia into an attack on 8 December 1980.

The first assault into N'Djamena did not end well. The FAN fought back bitterly, using a small number of RPG-7s captured during earlier fighting to destroy some twenty Libyan vehicles and, deploying captured SA-7s, they shot down at least one LAAF Mi-25 during the first assault into the city. Then, on the 12 December, the Libyans brought in several batteries of D-30 and M-46 artillery pieces that fired more than 10,000 shells into N'Djamena, while the LAAF supported this bombardment with SF.260s and Tu-22 bombers. The destruction of the Chadian capital was massive, with entire streets being burned-out, all telecommunications to the outside world, all gas stations, water and electric services destroyed. Most of the embassies, already evacuated before the onslaught, were demolished, while the number of civilian casualties remains unknown even today. However, the weeklong shelling of the city soon began showing its effects. After Habré escaped to Cameroon, in early December, the FAN fought only rear-guard battles until 15 December, when survivors escaped in the direction of Abéche and then into Sudan.

At least on paper, Gaddafi, Azziz and Radwan's operation, which included the stunning logistical accomplishment of deploying 5,000 troops with 500 vehicles, dozens of artillery pieces, a LAAF contingent of helicopter gunships and some light strike aircraft, together with the required supplies from the Aouzou Strip over 1,300 kilometres to N'Djamena, within a month, finally achieved the Libyans' goals. However, in traditional Chadian fashion, their joy was not to last long. Although Gaddafi managed to force Oueddei to agree to a merger of the two countries during a meeting in Tripoli on 6 January 1981, as soon as the new Chadian president was back in his ruined capital, he denounced the union. Within weeks, the GUNT was practically at war with 15,000 Libyan troops deployed in the country. Libya then found itself facing a new, much more powerful opponent than ever before.

CHAPTER 5
FON OVER SYRTE

Relations between Libya under Gaddafi's rule and the USA gradually worsened after Tripoli's announcement that the Gulf of Syrte (known as the 'Gulf of Sidra' in the USA) would be considered as Libyan territorial waters. In the spring 1974, Washington issued a diplomatic protest calling this announcement 'unacceptable' and a 'violation of international law', but otherwise did nothing to challenge Libyan claims, de facto accepting them as such. In fact, preoccupied with other issues, successive US administrations had several times rejected Pentagon proposals for large scale 'freedom of navigation' (FON) exercises designed to assert US rights in the gulf and illustrate Libyan inability to back up the claim with military force. Therefore, and because LAAF interceptors vigorously patrolled the area, even US and French reconnaissance aircraft that operated along Libyan borders tended to stay well away from the area, with few exceptions.

The situation changed once Ronald Reagan was elected into the White House in early 1981. Reagan wasted no time in increasing defence spending, developing a tougher policy towards the Soviet Union and its allies and announcing his intention to combat international terrorism. The latter decision brought Washington on a direct collision course with Tripoli. Libya was recognised as a 'genuine threat' to US interests in the Middle East and Africa, supporting up to 30 different terrorist organisations world-wide, and deploying operatives and agents of its intelligence services to assassinate the Libyan opposition in the USA. Correspondingly, Reagan's administration began developing plans to confront the Libyan claim over for Gulf of Syrte, undermine Gaddafi's domestic power base, thwart the Libyan position in Chad and decrease its influence in the Middle East and Africa. Only one month into his presidency, Reagan approved an assertive, comprehensive FON program, including exercises inside the Gulf of Syrte.[41]

Incidents and Non-Affairs

Even before Ronald Reagan took over as President of the USA, a series of incidents including, or apparently including, LAAF aircraft took place in the skies over the Mediterranean Sea. The first, and certainly the least known occurred in 1978. At that time the AdA was deploying its Douglas DC-8 Sarique ELINT/SIGINT gathering aircraft from Electronic Squadron 51 'Aubrac' (Escadre Electronique, EE) to fly a series of reconnaissance missions over and around several African countries allied with the USSR, in order to find details about the extent of their recently established radar networks. In the course of one such mission flown, on 16 May 1978, a Sarigue crossed much of Libya using gaps within the LAAF's radar network and without being intercepted, before continuing for Kinshasa in Zaire.

The number of such incidents increased significantly during 1980. On 23 March, two LAAF Mirage 5s opened fire on an Atlantic of the Aéronavale that was flying over the Mediterranean Sea off the Libyan coast. The crew of the French plane skilfully avoided this attack and nobody on board was injured.[42]

Another incident involving Libyan Air Force aircraft occurred on 27 June 1980. Late in the evening, a Douglas DC-9-15 airliner (registration I-TIGI, c/n 45724), Flight Number 870, operated by the Italian company Itavia Airlines was on en route from Guglielmo Marconi Airport in Bologna to Palermo International Airport in Sicily. It mysteriously disappeared while flying over the Tyrrhenian Sea, together with 81 crew members and passengers. While sadly such catastrophic accidents with passenger aircraft occur several times every year, the reasons for most of them are found thanks to excellent investigation methods developed over the last 40 years. However, this was not the case with Flight 870.

During the subsequent search and rescue (SAR) operations initiated by the Italian military even before the civilian authorities knew that the DC-9 was missing, and which lasted several days, floating debris and 38 bodies were recovered from an area of several hundred square kilometres. It took a number of years for the evidence to be compiled and be made available for the reconstruction of this tragedy. During that time, the investigation became mired by an unusual series of problems and not a few controversies. Even 30 years later, no official explanation or final report has been provided by the Italian government. Although most of the external fuselage of the Itavia DC-9 was subsequently recovered from the bottom of the Tyrrhenian Sea, and reconstructed, foreign experts concluded that the aircraft was probably destroyed by a bomb planted near the rear toilet. The Italian authorities, and the public in general, prefer to believe one of many conspiracy theories that has since emerged. Several of these are related to the crash of a LAAF MiG-23MS interceptor on Mount Sila, in Calabria, southern Italy, on 18 July 1980. Inside the cockpit of the crashed aircraft, Italian authorities found the body of its pilot, 1st Lt Ezzedin Koal. Reports about various military radars tracking up to nine different aircraft in the same part of the sky around the time Flight 870 passed through it, resulted in theories emberging that the DC-9 and the MiG were shot down in the course of air combat, supposedly involving up to

Usually operated from RAF Mildenhall, in Great Britain, but also from Souda Bay on Crete, RC-135Ws of the USAF flew dozens of ELINT/SIGINT reconnaissance sorties along Libyan borders in the 1970s and 1980s. Several times their crew found themselves exposed to attacks by Libyan interceptors, until the US Navy received an order to start escorting them by F-14 Tomcats. (Photo by Marinus Dirk Tabak)

seven other aircraft of Italian, French, US or even Israeli origin.[43] Whatever might have caused the crash of the Itavia DC-9, Hazem al-Bajigni's recollection about reasons for the crash of Koal's MiG-23 in Italy is quite clear:

> After recovering from my injuries suffered during an incident in 1977, I did a short stint at Sebha AB, where I flew SF.260s. By 1979 I was back to Benina AB and the next year I was assigned to fly MiG-23BNs with No. 1070 Squadron from al-Abraq AB, west of Tobruk, which was actually still under construction. The other two MiG-23BN-units of the LAAF – No. 1050 and No. 1060 – were still at Benina. Koal was a Syrian air force pilot, assigned to one of two MiG-23MS-squadrons at Benina, exclusively manned by Syrians. We could not fly with them because they used Arabic language while flying, while we used English. So, we flew in the morning and they in the afternoons and evenings (they had their own way of life too, so we did not mix much with them, though I did some socialising with their squadron leader, mainly out of curiosity). Koal was a young pilot on a regular training mission. His aircraft was unarmed and carried no extra fuel tanks. He has got a new breathing mask that day. Our subsequent investigation has shown that this mask was a too big. When he climbed to an altitude above 5,000 metres, he forgot to activate 100% oxygen and went into hypoxia. His wingman called him several times, but Koal was not responsive. His head slumped down when he was last seen and all efforts to communicate with him failed. His MiG, set to semi-auto-pilot (activated by a green button on the control stick) was set at 'straight and level' mode, so it just went on. Eventually, it crashed in Italy after running out of fuel. The crash report we've got from the Italian authorities did not indicate any kind of collision or combat damage of any kind.[44]

41 Stanik, pp. 32–44.

42 Agnès Saal, 'Chronologie des faits internationaux d'ordre juridique – 1980', *Annuaire francais de droit international*, Vol. 26, 1980, pp. 978–1040.

43 AviationSafetyNet.com; Frank Taylor, *A Case History Involving Wreckage Analysis* (Cranfield University, updated edition, 2006); various reports in contemporary Italian newspapers; 'The Mystery of Flight 870', *The Guardian*, 21 July 2006; Italian Court: Missile caused 1980 Mediterranean plane crash; 'Italy must pay compensation', *Washington Post/AP*, 23 Jan. 2013; Victor Ostrovsky, *The Other Side of Deception* (ISBN 978-0-06-109352-4).

44 The Italian authorities confirmed that Koal's MiG-23 was unarmed and 'without extra fuel tanks', when it crashed into Mount Sila. The Libyan government later issued an official statement citing that the plane was on a routine training mission in international air space over the Mediterranean when the pilot, 'apparently had a heart attack'. According to the same statement, the aircraft then, 'maintained speed, direction and altitude until running out of fuel', see *AW&ST*, 28 July 1980.

Mirage 5DE interceptors operated by No. 1003 Squadron LAAF were involved in several incidents with US and French reconnaissance aircraft flying off the Libyan coast in 1980. This rare photograph shows an example already wearing the national insignia introduced following the war with Egypt in July 1977. (Albert Grandolini Collection)

While Koal's loss therefore did not stand-up in relation to the 'Ustica Massacre' (as that case is known in Italy), the LAAF interceptors did become involved in at least two other incidents with foreign aircraft that occurred during the same year. At an unknown date, the same DC-8 of the EE.51 that had flown the mission 'across Libya' in 1978, was intercepted by two Libyan MiG-25P interceptors while underway over the central Mediterranean. LAAF ground control ordered both MiGs back to their base after Colonel Michel Gambs, the pilot of the Sarique, changed his course towards the north. However, the Number 2 in the Libyan formation ignored this order. He manoeuvred his MiG beneath and then in front of the DC-8, before engaging afterburners. Gambs commented:

I still recall, vividly, the terrific crescendo caused by his afterburners and shock-waves that almost caused us to lose control over our aircraft.[45]

Another incident of a similar type occurred on 16 September 1980, though this time involving an USAF Boeing RC-135 SIGINT/ELINT reconnaissance aircraft and two LAAF MiG-25s. Libyan pilots first approached the US plane and signalled the crew to turn away from what they considered to be the Libyan border. When the Americans ignored their signals, one of the MiGs fired a single air-to-air missile, though this missed its target (probably decoyed by deployment of electronic countermeasures). Five days later, on 21 September 1980, five Mirage 5s intercepted an RC-135 while it was flying 200 miles off the Libyan coast. However, this time the reconnaissance aircraft was escorted by three Grumman F-14A Tomcats from the aircraft carrier USS *John F Kennedy (CV-67),* and they managed to force the Libyans away without opening fire.

Some of such, rather nervous, Libyan actions were related to rumours about another failed coup attempt against Gaddafi, that was reportedly plotted by nineteen military officers during the fall of 1980. Hazem al-Bajigni subsequently found himself accused of intending to steal a C-130 transport and fly the plotters out of the country. Eventually, he was forced to flee in quite a spectacular fashion:

I fled to Crete on 11 February 1981. My defection was marred by technical problems and fiascos with the NATO Southern Command. Early on after taking off from Benina AB, I made a mistake. While escaping from Libya, I flew much too fast at much too low an altitude. A MiG-23 can sweep its wings to fly faster, but there is a limit of what the aircraft structure can support. If it is flown too fast with wings fully swept back while underway at low altitude, the swivelling mechanism would be damaged and the wings could not be moved forward. While flying away from Libya I accelerated to Mach 1.5 while underway at less than 100 feet (30m). This caused structural damage. I was planning to land at Iraklion AB, on Crete. But, arriving there, I found it covered by clouds. I circled several times flying low, right over the top of buildings, simply trying to get some attention. All the time I used the international frequency of 121.50MHz, calling for help. But, there was no answer (NATO was later very embarrassed about this). There were a few military jets flying in that general area, some looked like A-6s, but I could not intercept them to communicate with their crews because of my damaged wings. It's a long story, but eventually I got the wings to go forward to the landing configuration and ended up crash landing into the bushes at a remote site. This turned out to be the old, disused airfield of Maleme, famous from the times of World War II. I attempted to eject while doing so, but my seat did not work. Once outside of the aircraft I found myself all alone with nobody around. This was another hard-to-believe blunder by the local NATO force.

Although the wreckage of al-Bajigni's aircraft was returned to Libya three days later, tensions in the airspace along the northern Libyan borders remained high all through 1981.

Reagan's Rules of Engagement
US planning for the FON in the Gulf of Syrte lasted several months, and received Reagan's official go-ahead only on 1 August 1981. One of the reasons for the lengthy preparations for what would otherwise be considered a routine, peace-time live-firing exercise, run several times a year by different elements of the US military deployed around the world, was the Libyan record of attacking US aircraft in international airspace. Another was the development of new 'Rules of Engagement' (ROEs), designed to grant on-scene commanders the authority 'to counter either the use of force or an

45 Michel Gambs, *Les Missions de l'EE.0051* (unpublished summary about operational sorties by AdA's DC-8s).

Table 2: CVW-17 and CVW-8 during FON/OOMEX in August 1981

Aircraft Carrier	Carrier Air Wing & Squadrons	Aircraft Type & Modex	Duration of the Cruise
USS Forrestal (CV-59)	CVW-17	(AA)	2 March 1981–15 September 1981
	VF-74 Be-Devillers	F-4J AA100	
	VMFA-115 Fighting Silver Eagles	F-4J AA200	
	VA-83 Rampagers	A-7E AA300	
	VA-81 Sunliners	A-7E AA400	
	VA-85 Black Falcons	A-6E & KA-6D AA500	
	VAW-125 Tigertails	E-2C AA010	
	VAQ-130 Scorpions	EA-6B AA600	
	VS-30 Zappers	S-3A AA700	
	HS-3 Tridents	SH-3H AA730	
USS Nimitz (CVN-68)	CVW-8		3 August 1981–12 February 1982
	VF-41 Black Aces	F-14A AJ100	
	VF-84 Jolly Rogers	F-14A AJ200	
	VA-82 Marauders	A-7E AJ300	
	VA-86 Sidewinders	A-7E AJ400	
	VA-35 Black Panthers	A-6E & KA-6D AJ500	
	VAW-124 Bear Aces	E-2C AJ010	
	VMAQ-2 Det. Y	EA-6B CY610	
	VS-24 Scouts	S-3A AJ700	
	HS-9 Sea Griffins	SH-3H AJ730	
	HS-1 Det.4 Seahorses	SH-3G AR700	

immediate threat of the use of force' (so-called 'Reagan ROEs'), and even to pursue the possible attacker into the Libyan airspace. In the words of Lawrence 'Music' Muczynski, then an F-14 pilot assigned to the squadron VF-41 'Black Aces' of the US Navy:

The ROEs were very specific until then. We could not shoot without permission. Even if we were fired upon, we still had to call back to the ship, describe the situation and get permission to shoot. That was just a way too long. However, prior to this exercise we were briefed on new ROEs. We could now be pre-cleared by our controllers to engage a specific target, and most importantly, if we were fired on we could return fire, no questions asked. They developed this ROE due to the fact that during this exercise Lockheed EP-3 Orions, Grumman EA-6B Prowlers and Grumman E-2C Hawkeyes, and other high-value assets would all be present.[46]

Furthermore, the White House and the Pentagon wanted to stage a tremendous demonstration of US military power and send a clear signal about their altered policy to Gaddafi. Finally, the US Navy needed some time to concentrate two carrier battle groups, centred around the carriers USS *Forrestal (CV-59),* with Carrier Air Wing 17 (CVW-17) on board, and USS *Nimitz (CVN-69),* with CVW-8 embarked, with thirteen escort and support ships, including the nuclear-powered cruisers, USS *Texas (CGN-39)* and USS *Mississippi*

46 Muczynski, *Tomcat Sunset Symposium*, Oceana, Sept. 2006; this and all subsequent quotations from Muczynski are based on his presentation during the same symposium.

(CGN-40), in the Mediterranean Sea.[47]

The FON and the Open Ocean Missile Exercise (OOMEX) were announced on time to the Libyan authorities, and they immediately protested, calling them a violation of Libya's territorial waters and airspace. Nevertheless, the two carrier battle groups, under the command of Rear Admiral James E Service, moved to a position north of the Gulf of Syrte and commenced the exercise in the early hours of 18 August 1981.

While the missile exercise was going on, both carriers remained fully prepared to intercept any Libyan aircraft and naval vessels that approached the exercise area. Correspondingly, a number of McDonnell Douglas F-4J Phantom II and Grumman F-14A Tomcat interceptors were catapulted into the morning sky and positioned so as to establish a barrier between the exercise area and the Libyan coast. Supported by Grumman E-2C Hawkeye airborne early warning (AEW) aircraft, pairs of F-14s filled four stations and pairs of F-4s three, with one of the Tomcat stations being clearly south of 32° 30', which the Libyans declared as a northern border of their territory. At dawn, the Tomcats were followed by destroyers USS *William V Pratt (DDG-44)* and USS *Caron (DD-970),* which steamed south of 32° 30' and were to remain inside the Gulf of Syrte for the following 36 hours.

Over the Line of Death

When the US Navy-run FON in the Gulf of Syrte began, Gaddafi was on a state visit to Aden in the then South Yemen. Because the airspace where the US exercise took place was within the

47 Stanik, pp. 46–47.

responsibility of the flight control in Tripoli, as soon as USN aircraft appeared there, the Libyans requested the Americans to identify themselves. The Americans not only ignored such requests but then also entered the airspace south of the 'Line of Death'. Members of the RCC therefore ordered the LAAF to scramble and either force US Navy aircraft away or shot them down.[48] Correspondingly, no less than 35 pairs of Libyan interceptors, including a total of 70 MiG-23MS's, MiG-25Ps, Mirage F.1s, and even Su-22s, Su-22Ms and MiG-25RBs, approached the exercise area during 18 August 1981, as recalled by Muczynski:

> Fighters from Nimitz were responsible for three combat air patrol (CAP) stations, one to the south and two to the west of the exercise area. The Forrestal had two CAPs to the east of the shoot area. Both air wings also maintained a CAP over their respective carrier. On the first day of the exercise all three of our CAPs were engaged. The perception was that the two western CAPs were getting most of the action.

While some of LAAF pilots did their best in attempting to bring one of the US Navy fighters within range of their weapons, most did not show any kind of aggressive intentions at all. According to Libyan accounts, the major reason for this was that, timely warned by E-2C Hawkeyes and supported by electronic countermeasures emitted by Grumman EA-6B Prowlers and EP-3 Orions, the excellently trained Americans entered every engagement from a favourable position. They could usually position their fighters 'in the saddle', behind, above or below LAAF aircraft, in the best position to deny them a chance of successful engagement and force them to withdraw. Muczynski explained:

> Half of the time we would intercept them and they would let us join right to the wing. One Tomcat would stay in a mile trail, just in case, while the wingman would take pictures, inspect the MiGs visually, and 'communicate' (make rude hand gestures) to the Libyan pilots. It was pretty surreal to approach just a couple of feet from two MiG-25s. Until then it was just a picture in a book, and now here it was next to my jet. And when he lit those huge afterburners on that Foxbat, wow! His motors were huge! He could really move in a straight line, but couldn't do much else.

Not knowing that their opponents received an order to 'destroy' any US Navy aircraft underway south of 30° 32', US Navy pilots like Cdr 'Bad Fred' Lewis had mixed it up with successive pairs of Libyan fighters. Only in three cases did the Libyans manage to penetrate the exercise zone, forcing Americans to stop their OOMEX. From the standpoint of American fliers, the situation was resembling scenes from their dissimilar air combat training, as recalled by one of VF-84's pilots:

> On 18th August, it was mostly fun and games, well, mostly. Let's just say that ever since then, I know exactly what a Mirage F.1 looks like from a distance of 600–800 ft (200–400 metres) as it pulls lead for guns.[49]

Fast Eagles versus Fitters

The situation was to experience a dramatic change early the next morning. Around 6:00am local time on 19 August 1980, six F-14s and four F-4s, supported by two E-2Cs, took off towards their

48 Ali Tani, interview, July 2001.
49 'Gizmo', interview, Oct. 2002.

Some of the first LAAF fighters to approach the aircraft of the US Navy's 6th Fleet on 18 August were these two MiG-25R reconnaissance fighters from No. 1035 Squadron (note the squadron identification unusually applied on the front fuselage of the MiG in foreground). (USN)

Top view at the LAAF MiG-25R serial number 504, which was the second of two intercepted on the same occasion. Notable is that this aircraft also had the unit designation stencilled on its front fuselage. (USN)

Soviet-made MiG-23MS, like this example with serial number 9082, were particularly interesting for USN pilots. Unknown at that time was the fact that this was one of only a handful of LAAF MiG-23Ms modified with compatibility to carry R-13M missiles on underwing hardpoints, one of which can be seen clearly on this photograph. (USN)

A pair of LAAF MiG-23Ms, serial numbers 9071 (foreground, upper right corner) and 9219, both of which were armed with R-13Ms on underwing stations, in addition to old R-3S installed on underfuselage hardpoints. (USN)

Probably the best known photograph of LAAF aircraft taken on 18 August 1981, was this example, showing the MiG-23MS with serial number 6916. Equipped with the weapon system of the MiG-21, complex to maintain and problematic to fly, the aircraft proved a great disappointment during its early service in Libya. (USN)

A wonderful study of the MiG-23MS with serial number 8702, armed with old R-3S missiles. The aircraft was operated by either No. 1050 or No. 1060 Squadron, both of which were based at Benina AB and entirely crewed by Syrians as of August 1981. (USN)

Another less-well known photograph from 18 August 1981 is this MiG-23MS with serial number 8938. It wore the same, standardised camouflage pattern as all other aircraft of this type delivered to Libya. Apparently, the serial numbers of LAAF MiG-23s at that time consisted of the 'last four' of their construction number. (USN)

While attracting a lot less public attention than Nimitz's Tomcats, F-4Js from USS Forrestal actually intercepted more than 50% of LAAF fighters that approached the ships of the 6th Fleet on 18 August 1981. Here a Phantom from VF-74 BeDevillers is escorting a MiG-23MS away. (USN)

Top view of an unknown LAAF MiG-23MS intercepted by USN fighters on 18 August 1981, showing details of the camouflage pattern and national markings to advantage. (USN)

Comparing their notes during post-mission de-briefs, USN pilots concluded that the training of Libyans they encountered varied greatly, with those flying Mirage F.1s being 'markedly superior' to the pilots flying Soviet-built aircraft. Accordingly, Mirage pilots were more difficult to intercept and sufficiently skilful at evasive action and preventing USN aircraft from holding close formation. This example (serial 515) was the only one the Americans managed to photograph. (USN)

patrol stations. As on the previous day, the southernmost of these was inside the airspace claimed by Libyans. After Hawkeyes and fighters, USS Nimitz and USS Forrestal launched a similar number of Lockheed S-3A Vikings and Vought A-7E Corsair IIs to search for two Soviet submarines known to have been in the area and also keep an eye on Libyan Navy ships that were expected to approach.

The southernmost patrol station was occupied by two Tomcats from VF-41: call-sign Fast Eagle 102 (F-14A BuAerNo 160403) flown by the squadron CO, Commander Henry 'Hank' Kleemann, with Lt David 'DJ' Venlet as radar intercept officer (RIO), while Fast Eagle 107 (F-14A BuAerNo 160390) was flown by Lt Muczynski, with RIO Lt JG James 'Amos' Anderson. Once airborne, both Tomcats topped up their tanks from a Grumman KA-6D Intruder tanker and then reported to one of the E-2Cs that they were about to reach their patrol station. After establishing a 'race-track' pattern, in which one of the two aircraft is always heading in the direction of

the threat axis, the two crews waited, not really expecting anything to happen in the area. Muczynski continued:

I was involved in several intercepts of Libyan fighters on the previous day and would have had no problem if nothing happened on that morning. Prior to my launch, we did a weapons check and it turned out that my station 8A [right 'shoulder' station for AIM-9 Sidewinder air-to-air missiles] did not function. My Tomcat was armed with two AM-9L Sidewinders and two AIM-7F Sparrows, but this meant that only three of these, plus the M-61A1 Vulcan cannon, were operational. We reached our station at sunrise. On previous day it was very quiet there and that morning nothing was going on. We started making our circles in the sky while listening on the radio as two other Tomcats from our squadron were intercepting two Libyan MiG-25s. I also heard from two A-7s that a Libyan Osa missile boat was active in the area. Several minutes later, the E-2C ordered two Be-Devillers' [VF-74's] F-4s to intercept a pair of MiG-23s.

Around 7:15am it was still dark and we were short of preparing to return to our carrier. Dave [Venlet] detected a contact in a southerly direction, some 80 miles (128 kilometres) away, climbing to our altitude of 20,000ft [6,100m] and heading in our direction. The E-2C called almost at the same time and reported that the bogey was moving very fast, some 540kts (995km/h), in a northerly direction and directly towards Fast Eagle 102. As we headed towards the contact, Amos acquired the same target with our radar, while I gained some 6,000–8,000ft (1,800–2,400m) of altitude off Hank's wing to obtain a better position from which to begin the interception.

In this fashion, the Tomcats tried to 'sidestep' to gain lateral separation from the incoming Libyan fighter in order to be well placed to turn behind it and 'merge', when the two formations met. Once Kleeman engaged the bogey, Muczynski was to pull up and provide protection. In turn, this formation also caused not a little confusion for the Libyan ground controllers, due to the distance between their radars and the Tomcats. Their radars were showing only one target, usually the lower one (Kleemann's aircraft), to which they were vectoring their fighters – to the advantage of the Americans. Muczynski continued:

The plan didn't quite function when each time we jinked to the side, the Libyans, vectored by their ground control, turned into us and neutralised the angle. We jinked twice but couldn't reach an advantageous position and thus accelerated to 550kts (1000km/h) while turning directly into Libyans. I maintained my position off Hank's wing and monitored the developments. I still didn't expect an air combat and called Amos to ready his camera, like the day before. When the range decreased to nine miles (fifteen km), my radar malfunctioned. I was frustrated and swore to myself: first the 8A station, now the radar.

With a relative closing rate of 1,100kts the opponents approached each other in a matter of seconds, the single blip on AWG-9 radar screen transforming into a pair of LAAF fighter-bombers:

At approximately eight miles (thirteen km) I saw the two Su-22 Fitter Js on the nose (i.e. dead ahead). They were flying a formation we refer to as welded wing, within about 150ft (50m) of each other.[50]

Although the Su-22s and Su-22Ms encountered by USN pilots on the previous day were all armed with either R-3S or more advanced R-13M air-to-air missiles, and had two internal 30mm cannons installed in their wing roots, they were no match for F-14s in air combat. The 'Fitter' was much less manoeuvreable and its heavy cockpit framing limited the view out of the cockpit. Pulling 7Gs to the left, Muczynski started to position himself behind the Libyans:

Hank called to say there were two Libyan Su-22s in welded wing. Because of all the manoeuvring I ended up back at his four o'clock and about 5,000ft (1,524m) above him. I was looking

down into the early morning haze and I couldn't see them yet. At about four miles, I finally got a tally-two on them. Just then my radar died. We didn't know it at that time but the short range function had died, and there was nothing we were going to be able to do about it. They flew directly at Hank and probably never saw me. I rolled my wings and was screaming downhill so much I pulled the throttle to idle with the speed brakes out to keep from overshooting the merge.

At approximately 7:18am, the pilot leading a pair of Su-22Ms from Syrte-based No. 1032 Squadron LAAF radioed to his wingman, 'I'm preparing to fire!' and, second later: 'I've fired!' These transmissions were heard and recorded by the crew of one of several US ELINT/SIGINT reconnaissance aircraft operational in the area, and left no doubts about Libyan intentions.[51] Already in a 150-degree turn to the left, Kleemann recalled the shocking sight:

The pass (was) nose to nose, with No. 102 (Kleemann's Tomcat) very nearly on the flight path with the two Fitters. I rolled my wings and began a (left) turn to keep the Fitters in sight and turn around and rendezvous on them. About 500ft (150m) above them and 1,000ft (300m) out in front, I observed a missile being fired from the right station of the Fitter. As I saw the missile come off, I communicated to my wingman that we had been fired at. I then continued a very hard turn across their tails to come back and find them. I kept both of them in sight through this manoeuvre. The lead Fitter did a climbing left-hand turn in the general direction of my wingman. I initially turned around to go after the man who had fired, as I saw my wingman come in. He came into view in front of me, starting to come into a position behind the lead Fitter as he continued off in that direction. Since I saw that he had him under control, I switched my attention to the wing Fitter who had done a climbing right-hand turn.

Fired from such a close range and a head-on aspect of only 20–25 degrees, the missile launched by the lead Su-22M never had a chance of even guiding to its target, and even less so of scoring a hit. Muczynski vividly recalled the scene:

It was still dark and I clearly saw the whole left side of the lead Su-22 lighting up. There was a bright orange flash and then a smoke trail. There was never any doubt about this being a jettisoned drop tank: that Libyan fired a missile! Hank was less than 1,000ft (300m) from the Fitters when the missile went under him, then kind of came up towards us before clearing off behind us. It sure got my full attention. This is where the old adage of 'train as you fight, cause you'll fight like you trained' came into play. After the thousands of intercepts in training, everything now just became automatic. Break turn, chaff and flares, all just happened. I rolled back and kept the visual, and instinctively pulled right to the 6.5 G limit of the aircraft while coming down on the intercept. Hank called on the radio to report that we are under fire and ordered me: 'You go for the guy that shot at us, I'm going for the wingman'.

In accordance with their ROEs, the two Tomcat crews were now granted permission to take immediate action and defend themselves. Without hesitation, they went after their opponents with the intention to return fire. The two Libyans meanwhile entered a standard Soviet-style combat manoeuvre called 'shells'. Designed as defence against an attack from the rear hemisphere,

50 Spick, F-14, p. 60; this and all subsequent quotations from Kleemann are based on same source. Tragically, Commander Kleemann was killed on 3 Dec. 1985, while landing an F/A-18A Hornet at NAS Miramar in rain. His aircraft aqua plained and turned turtle, hitting the ground with the top of the cockpit first. Ironically, at that time Kleemann was the officer responsible for the conduct of the F-14 programme and expected to push many of the related projects much ahead.

51 Stanik, p. 54.

Successful crews of Fast Eagle 102 (from left to right) James Anderson and Lawrence Muczynksi, and Fast Eagle 107A with Henry Kleemann and David Venlet in front of the F-14A 'AJ-107', as seen in Naples a few days after the clash of 19 August 1981. (USN)

David Venlet (left) and Henry Kleeman reconstructing the clash with Libyan Su-22s for the press. (USN)

'Fast Eagle 102' the F-14A Block 95 flown by the CO VF-41, Cdr Henry Hank Kleemann and Lt (later Admiral) David 'DJ' Venlet that was the lead of the two Tomcats and the first to score during the short air battle on the morning of 19 August 1981. The aircraft was subsequently re-serialled to 'AJ101' and became Kleemann's 'personal' plane for the rest of that memorable cruise. (USN)

Close-up of the cockpit section of the F-14A 'AJ102', showing the detail of the original 'kill marking' applied following Kleemann's kill against a Libyan Su-22, on 19 August 1981. (Photo by Don Jay, via von Broekhuisen)

this envisaged each formation member flying a slant, looping in the opposite direction. The manoeuvre did not function because the Tomcats were in much too good a position and too close. Kleemann followed the Libyan wingman through his right-hand turn:

My Fitter was approaching the sun. As I intended to use a Sidewinder heat-seeking missile, I realised that that was not a good position to shoot from. I waited about ten seconds until he cleared the sun, (then) fired my missile. There was no chance that I wasn't going to pull the trigger. It did go through my mind that it was likely to cause a ruckus, but I had no choice. The missile guided, struck him in his tailpipe area causing him to lose control of the airplane and he ejected within about five seconds.

Going for the Su-22M that fired at Kleemann, Muczynski quickly brought his Tomcat into a firing position:

The F-14 had incredible superiority in the turn rate and radius over the Su-22, especially because we flew the F-14A Block 95 model with the auto-manoeuvring slats and flaps, which worked phenomenally well. This allowed us to run the wings in the auto mode, and the wing sweep was automatically managed to maintain the best manoeuvrability for any speed. While Hank went after the Libyan wingman, we had gotten behind and below our guy, and I'm trying all kinds of things to get a radar lock, which was never going to happen. Finally, I decided to pull the nose up and get a boresight AIM-9 seeker lock. I'm just getting all this done

when Jim in my backseat says, 'Someone's been hit, someone's been shot!' So I ask, 'Who is it?' He says, 'I can't tell'. Because of the split of the two bandits, we were several miles from the other engagement, and Jim said all he could see was flame and smoke. Since I'd got my bandit trapped at twelve o'clock I had the time to take my eyes off it and look over to the east. Sure enough, Jim was right! All I could see was smoke and a black dot.

Many thoughts went through my mind during those seconds. Such as, even though we know the ROEs, we are not at war. If I shoot my guy and Hank decides not to do so, boy I would be in a world of trouble if the skipper holds off and I don't. And with unpredictable Gaddafi, this could start World War Three. I was wrestling with all of this for a nanosecond, and I get on the radio and ask Hank, 'What should I do with this guy?' Hank, who had lost sight of us while shooting his guy, was concerned my bandit may have switched back onto them and they were at risk. So, instead of responding to my question he makes it very clear, the most brilliant radio call I have ever heard, 'Shoot, shoot, shoot!'

I've got the master arm on, and am just about to squeeze the trigger on this guy when he starts a hard, maybe 5–6 G turn to the right. I don't think he knew we were there; we were below and behind and didn't have a radar to trigger his warning gear. So, he starts his right turn and it's no problem staying with him, but I do have the issue with my only operational Sidewinder: if

Fin of the F-14A BuAerNo160403, after it was re-serialled as AJ101, with kill marking now in a new place. A few weeks later it was replaced by an 'E', a mark of VF-41 being distinguished by the US Navy's 'Battle E' praise too. (Photo by von Broekhuisen)

Left-hand view of the LAAF Su-22 serial number 5814, as seen on the afternoon of 18 August 1981. It remains unknown whether this variant, distinguishable by the large undernose housing for a laser-marker, or the more streamlined Su-22M was involved in the clash with USN Tomcats, on the morning of 19 August 1981. (USN)

A near-top view of the same aircraft (LAAF Su-22 serial number 5814). Interestingly, and contrary to slightly more advanced Su-22Ms sighted on the same day, this aircraft was armed with two R-13M air-to-air missiles. (USN)

this Sidewinder wouldn't work, I would have to go in and gun this guy. So, with about 5 G's on my jet, I squeeze the trigger and out of my peripheral vision to the left, I see the missile come off the rail. However, because I was turning right, the missile went straight for 1,000 feet after launch, apparently going away to the left from me. I could not believe my eyes: first the 8A station, then radar, now the missile going stupid! So, I switch to the guns wondering about the reasons for the missile malfunction, when the Sidewinder unlocked the fins, pulled 45 G's and flashed by, right in front of my windscreen to the right! As fast as I could get

my eyes back to the right the missile tracked right up the tail pipe, and the explosion was just like in WWII gun camera film: massive explosion, with smoke, parts and tanks flying everywhere, directly in front of me, less than half a mile away. My immediate thought was, 'Oh God, I've just shot myself down!' I took both hands on the stick and buried it in my lap, pulling as hard as I could, my neck hurt for days after this. Once back on USS Nimitz, one of our senior maintenance Master Chiefs pulled me aside and asked if I thought I might have over-G'd the airplane. After thinking for a while, I told him that I might have. There is a tradition that if you over-G the jet, you help the technicians pull panels and do the inspection. So, I asked if they wanted me to help right away. He leaned in and said quietly, 'Well Sir, it was 10.2 G's, and I'm gonna give you a free one for doing a hell of a job today.'

After no debris hit us, I jammed the stick forward and rolled to the right. We were upside down looking up through the canopy at the ocean and the Su-22 below us. It was blown in half at the wing-root, and the forward half was tumbling end over end. There was fuel streaming out and smoke and fire everywhere, and parts and tanks were still falling away. Just then I saw the canopy came off and the little rocket under the seat as it cleared the wreckage. He got seat-man separation, but was just falling. We lost the sight of him and never saw a chute open.

This encounter had lasted about three minutes and 44 seconds, from the US pilots sighting the Sukhois for the first time until the second Su-22M was shot down, some 60 miles (110km) north of the Libyan coast. The two Tomcats rejoined their formation and turned north in the direction of USS Nimitz.

Foxbat Hunt

Four additional Tomcats vectored by E-2Cs to make sure Fast Eagle 102 and 107 were safe, found no other Libyan aircraft within the engagement area. Nevertheless, and despite the loss of two Su-22Ms, the LAAF continued sending fighters to challenge the Americans. Further intercepts thus followed barely an hour after Fast Eagles 102 and 107 had returned aboard USS Nimitz. A pilot from VF-84 recalled:

After the shoot-down of two Libyan Su-22s, it got really serious. F-14s that were holding station at 250 knots one day were suddenly maintaining 350–400 knots. Shortly after two Libyan Su-22s were shot down by a section led by CO of VF-41, Ed 'Hunyack' Andrews got airborne. He really wanted to shoot some Foxbats down.[52]

Andrews was paired with an F-14A from VF-41, flown by Lt 'Junior' Thomas, with Lt Cdr Paul Williamson as RIO. Williamson recalled:

We launched in good time and were vectored to a southeasterly station east of Misurata (the LAAF base), and joined with a fighter from our sister squadron VF-84. After a short time on station, we were vectored almost due west to intercept two high-speed, relatively high-altitude aircraft which appeared to have launched from Misurata. We acquired the aircraft on radar and completed the intercept, identifying the aircraft as Foxbats.

The two Foxbats in question were MiG-25Ps of No. 1015 Squadron LAAF, forward deployed at Misurata AB, and led by

52 'Gizmo', interview, Oct. 2002.

The appearance of R-3S-armed Su-22Ms was something of a surprise for USN fliers. This big and powerful fighter-bomber was not a very good interceptor and armed with air-to-air missiles for self-defence purposes only. (USN)

Another LAAF Su-22M intercepted on 18 August. Notable is a complete absence of serial numbers and armament consisting of two R-3S missiles. It is possible that some of the Libyan Su-22Ms were upgraded to Su-22M-2K by that time. (USN)

Major Khalid Maeena. Like his colleagues before, Maeena received the order to 'chase away' any US Navy aircraft he could find. His attempt did not work, since the American pilots did not notice any kind of particularly aggressive behaviour on the part of the Libyan pilots, as explained by Williamson:

> Naturally, we were excited, but the intercept and escort of the Foxbats was relatively routine. Upon intercept, they made a few mild 360 degrees turns and then appeared to be returning to base. We broke off, but then had to intercept them again when they steadied up on an easterly heading (i.e. towards the fleet). Eventually, they switched on their afterburners and departed, climbing to the west. I was impressed with the size and acceleration of the Foxbat, but because of its size, weight and wing configuration, I don't believe it would present much of a threat in a conventional turning fight. Its acceleration in afterburner is impressive, but understandable in view of its published high-altitude speed.[53]

Eventually, although remaining airborne for four hours, Andrews had to return without a kill. With their radars and communications jammed by electronic countermeasures, Maenaa and his wingman found it impossible to acquire any of US aircraft with their radars and could not attack.[54] Following their ROEs, US commanders did not grant permission to fire to any of the Tomcat pilots and shortly afterwards, Admiral Service concluded OOMEX and withdrew both carrier battle groups from the exercise area. Some excitement still existed after no less than 45 successive engagements with 90 different Libyan fighters over two days. As sundown on 19 August 1981 approached, the alert was sounded on both carriers:

> One of outlying ships detected two unidentified delta-winged aircraft that were heading towards Nimitz and since I was on Alert-15, I dashed madly to the flight deck to man and launch. A couple of minutes later, the alert was cancelled, when the 'unidentified aircraft' were identified as a pair of Phantoms from USSR Forrestal, that had gotten turned around.[55]

US Fame and Libyan Shame

With hindsight, it might appear hard to understand the importance of the entire FON exercise in the Gulf of Syrte and resulting aerial 'clashes' between the fliers of the US Navy and Libyan pilots. On paper, the downing of two Libyan Su-22s by two US Navy F-14s on 19 August 1981 was only the first, minor military victory in what was to develop into an undeclared US war on Libya. However, in the USA this victory generated an outburst of national pride and outright public euphoria. It also gave an immense morale booster to the US military that was still recovering from an 'honourable withdrawal' from Vietnam. This victory also improved the image and prestige of the USA and its military around the world, even gaining at least 'private' praise from Arab governments that publicly charged Washington with aggression against a fellow Arab nation.

At the tactical level, the US Navy proved that it drew many valuable lessons from the Vietnam War and spent much of the 1970s learning these. Its pilots had learned to manoeuvre their aircraft aggressively and fully exploit the built-in technology. The large investment in their training, especially that provided by the Naval Fighter Weapons School (better known under its popular name 'Top Gun'), paid off fully over the Gulf of Syrte. Ably supported by superior detection and systems for electronic countermeasures, Tomcat and Phantom pilots made extensive use of the highly flexible 'loose duce' formation and various tactical methods taught to them at Top Gun and relentlessly prosecuted every engagement in a disciplined yet aggressive fashion. In turn, by not opening fire when this was not necessary, they also proved to the politicians in Washington that they could depend upon the military to apply only the authorised amount of force.

In comparison, the Libyans could not look back on any similar experiences, but only depend on what they learned from their foreign instructors, of which only the French possessed any kind of fresh combat experience. Perhaps unsurprisingly, not only their skills, but also their aircraft and weaponry were jammed, and outmanoeuvred by the Americans. As could be expected after such experiences, the Libyan administration reacted with the usual vitriolic rhetoric and an outright disinformation campaign. The Jamahiriya Arab News Agency reported that the LAAF had fought eight F-14s and shot down one.[56] Amid wild rumours spreading through Tripoli, including that the CIA was planning to overthrow Gaddafi and that

53 Spick, F-14, p. 61.
54 Ali Tani, interview, July 2001.
55 'Gizmo', interview, Oct. 2002.

56 Stanik, p. 61.

The appearance of R-40RD-armed MiG-25Ps of the LAAF caused quite some excitement amongst US Navy fliers. This example, serial number 7708, was flown by the wingman of a pair intercepted barely two hours after two LAAF Su-22s were shot down on the morning of 19 August 1981. (USN)

The MiG-25P serial number 7708 survived nearly 20 years in service with No. 1035 Squadron LAAF before it was effectively abandoned on the tarmac of Um Aittitiqah AB ('Mitiga', former Wheelus AFB), as seen here. (Photo of Eddy de Krujif)

the US Navy fleet was about to assault Libya in conjunction with Egypt and Sudan, the Libyan media was busy maintaining morale by spreading fantastic reports about the success of the Libyan Air Force. The two downed Su-22 pilots were shown on the State TV, alive and well, later that evening, and then Maj Maeena appeared. He reported to have, 'personally chased six F-14 bombers that had been on their way to attack many Libyan cities'. He went on to, 'first, thank Libya's leader Gaddafi, and secondly, the people of the Soviet Union for supplying him with the MiG-25 that enabled him to defend his homeland from the American aggressors, and shoot down all six of them as they tried to land and hide on their carrier ship'.

However, such statements were little more than 'boasting for public relation purposes'. The LAAF pilots and their commanders understood very well that something went badly wrong, and that the Americans completely outclassed and outmanoeuvred them. After years of intensive training and the acquisition of very expensive weapons and support systems, this was extremely frustrating for many. Colonel Ali Tani, who led a pair of MiG-25Ps that ended up right in front of two old F-4Js on 18 August, explained:

Essentially, our Soviet aircraft were badly under-equipped electronically. Within one minute of receiving an initial intercept vector from our ground control, the EA-6Bs and EP-3s deployed by the US 6th Fleet in support of their interceptors had blinded our radars and muted our communications. From that moment on we were flying 'blind and deaf', completely dependent on our eyes for detecting Americans. Our radars were useless. We could neither see what's going on ahead of us, nor ask our ground control for another vector or advice. Our ground control could not listen to American radio transmissions. If we acquired anything with our radars, they would implant decoy radar signatures into our systems, which we would pick up as 'real' bogeys. We were successively sending our interceptors after fake targets only for our pilots to find nothing but F-4s and F-14s on their tails. These were traps to bring us to their turf, while we thought we were chasing a real target...

Big Unknown: Tolkachev Factor

The first reaction within the LAAF to such negative experiences was to blame the Soviets for delivery of inferior and obsolete aircraft, equipped with armament and electronics that could not match the US equipment. Unsurprisingly, the Libyans insisted Moscow provided more advanced arms. As so often when facing similar complaints from Arabs, the Soviet advisors in Libya reacted by blaming poor training of LAAF pilots and their lack of tactical skills for the fiasco.[57] Eventually, although the USSR subsequently did agree to provide at least limited amounts of more modern equipment, including advanced variants of MiG-25 interceptors, no satisfactory solution was ever found. However, considering what has become known about some of the developments in the background ever since, it is very likely that the Soviets were simply not in a position to provide anything 'better'.

There are strong indications that the successful paralysing of the LAAF by the US Navy was not exclusively based on superior training, experience and application of advanced technology, but at least as much on the acquisition and application of vastly superior intelligence.

Many Libyan emigrants and defectors that had left their country in the 1970s had provided the Americans with detailed insights into the condition, deployment, equipment, combat capabilities and readiness rates of the LAAF. Even more important, especially in regards to the obvious capability of the US Navy to deploy highly effective electronic countermeasures against even the most modern LAAF aircraft, was the fact that during the late 1970s the USA began acquiring vast amounts of first class intelligence directly from the Soviet Union. The source that provided this intelligence was none other than Adolf Georgievich Tolkachev, an electronics engineer who was working as one of the chief designers for the Scientific Research Institute of Radar (NIIR or NII Radar; meanwhile better known as Phazotron Design Bureau) – the Soviet Union's largest developer of military radars and avionics.

Motivated by persecution of his wife's parents under Joseph Stalin and disaffected by the communist government, starting in 1979, Tolkachev established ties to the US CIA in Moscow and began transferring endless volumes of highly classified and extremely sensitive data about most important avionic systems, radars and weapons systems installed in Soviet-made combat aircraft. The amount of material provided by him was such that the CIA translators

57 For numerous examples of such behaviour from both sides, see Cooper et al., *Arab MiGs Vols. 1–4*.

Libyan spokesperson pointing at the approximate place where the two LAAF Su-22s were shot down by two USN F-14s on 19 August 1981. (Albert Grandolini Collection)

Although Larry Muczynski saw the ejection of his opponent, he never saw the parachute of the Libyan pilot open. Nevertheless, the two downed Su-22-pilots were shown on Libyan TV on the evening of 19 August 1981. They can be seen on this photograph, encircled in black. (Albert Grandolini Collection)

The two downed Libyan Su-22-pilots were apparently recovered by SA.321 Super Frelon helicopters of the LAAF, like this example (coded LC-153), photographed in Malta several years earlier. (Albert Grandolini Collection)

In an attempt to bolster the morale of its armed forces and population, the LAAF flew a lot during the following days, showing even their Tu-22 bombers in public. These two were photographed while passing low over a beach near Tripoli. (Albert Grandolini Collection)

could not keep up with their task. Actually, US intelligence was busy translating and studying the information provided by Tolkachev well into the 1990s, years after he was revealed to the Soviets by one of their spies within the US intelligence community and arrested by the KGB in early 1985.

Although the CIA never published precise details about any of the systems in question, the information it did release emphasises 'extremely high customer satisfaction with Tolkachev's reporting'. By December 1979, the Defence Department had, 'completely reversed its direction on a multi-million dollar electronics package for one of its latest fighter aircraft'. One of the internal CIA evaluations from March 1980 praised Tolkachev's information on the latest generation of Soviet surface-to-air missile systems, stating: 'We never before obtained such detail and understanding of such systems until years after they were actually deployed.' In April 1980, another internal CIA memorandum called his information on jam-proofing tests for Soviet fighter aircraft radar systems 'unique'. Obviously, he provided data that was not obtainable by other technical means available to the Americans. Only a few months later, Tolkachev was credited with, 'providing unique information on a new Soviet fighter aircraft, and documents on several new models of airborne missile systems.' Similarly, a memorandum from the Defence Department from September 1980 praised the impact of Tolkachev's reporting as, 'limitless in terms of enhancing US military systems' effectiveness, and, 'in the potential to save lives and equipment ... instrumental in shaping the course of billions of dollars of US research and development activities.'[58]

This, as well as various other assessments based on what little the CIA did release about its cooperation with Tolkachev, points to the fact that he might have caused irreparable damage to the Soviet aviation industry. He certainly provided the Americans with a full insight into not only such modern Soviet-made aircraft as the MiG-29, MiG-31 or Sukhoi Su-27, but foremost enabled them to develop electronic countermeasures against these even before they entered

service during the first half of the 1980s. Therefore, it would be a little surprising if Tolkachev had failed to provide information of similar quality about older fighter aircraft like the MiG-23MS's or MiG-25P, their radars, avionics and weapons systems (including air-to-air missiles deployed from them), as these were in service with the LAAF of the early 1980s.

In summary, it is reasonably safe to conclude that in the course of the engagement with the US Navy over the Gulf of Syrte in August 1981, the Libyan Arab Air Force became the first victim of Tolkachev's treachery.

58 Bary G Royden, *Tolkachev, A Worthy Successor to Penkovsky: An Exceptional Espionage Operation*, CIA Center for the Study of Intelligence, Studies in Intelligence Vol. 47, No. 3, 14 Apr. 2007.

CHAPTER 6
SHOWDOWN IN CHAD

While the success of the US Navy's FON in the Gulf of Syrte practically collapsed the Libyan claim of exercising total control over that area, it was only one of the 'anti-Gaddafi' measures initiated by the Reagan administration. Under the impression that Gaddafi had

next showdown in Chad, with France also involved.[59]

Defeat of the Arab Cause
With the situation in Chad continuing to turn against Libyan

Libyan troops embarking on a LAAF Il-76 transport at N'Djamena IAP, during their excellently organised withdrawal in November 1981. (Albert Grandolini Collection)

ordered the launch of a campaign of bombardments of FAN bases in Sudan, the assassination of President Anwar as-Sadat of Egypt, the continued support of various terrorist organisations and even a threat to assassinate President Reagan, the White House set up additional plans for operations against Libya. While the US administration subsequently found itself distracted by developments in Grenada, Lebanon and elsewhere, parts of this plan eventually resulted in the

interests, and informed that the USA were covertly involved in the reconstruction of the FAN, in August 1981 Gaddafi ordered the LAAF to launch a bombardment of Habré's bases inside Sudan. The first of these attacks was flown by Tu-22s staging through Ma'atan Bishrar AB in southern Libya, but by September 1981, when work on lengthening the runway in Aouzou was complete, some were flown from north-western Chad. The Reagan administration

59 Stanik, p. 63.

Wreckage of the LAAF SF.260WL '341', shot down outside al-Junaina in Darfur, Sudan, on 16 September 1981. (Tom Cooper Collection)

From Autumn 1981, LAAF Tu-22s flew intensive operations against numerous targets, not only inside Chad but also in Sudan. On 20 September 1981, one of them dropped three FAB-500 bombs on Omdurman, attempting to hit a pro-FAN radio station in the second largest Sudanese city. (USN)

The relentless activity of the LAAF prompted the USA to several times deploy its E-3A Sentry AWACS to Egypt and Sudan, in the period 1981–1983. This Sentry was photographed while arriving at Cairo West AB in Egypt in 1982. (USAF)

All the deployments of USAF E-3s, F-15s and B-52s to Egypt were supported by the then most modern tanker aircraft of the US Air Force, the KC-10A Extender. This example was photographed at Cairo West AB, in 1982. (USAF)

reacted by establishing ties to President Jafar Muhammad Numayri of Sudan and announcing that the multinational exercise Bright Star '81, was to be held in Egypt in November of the same year, and would include US forces training together with those of Sudan, Somalia and Oman. Undeterred, the LAAF continued its attacks until one SF.260 was shot down by ground fire near Junaina in Darfur (western Sudan), on 16 September 1981, killing the crew of two. Gaddafi was so outraged by the loss that he ordered the Tu-22s to strike a radio station supportive of the FAN in Omdurman, the second largest city in Sudan. A sole bomber flew this mission four days later, dropping three FAB-500 bombs, all of which missed their actual target but flattened three civilian houses nearby, killing at least three and injuring twenty civilians in the process. Despite much international protest, the LAAF subsequently intensified similar operations, primarily through staging Tu-22s through a repaired and lengthened runway at Faya. By November 1981, at least twenty different villages and minor towns in Chad had been bombed, including Junaina, Kulbus, Tina, Tanduatu and Asognam, and hundreds of civilians killed or injured.

Meanwhile, prompted by Libyan and US military activities, France and the Organisation of African Unity (OAU) began exercising heavy pressure upon Libya, suggesting a replacement of Libyan Army units through a peace-keeping force consisting of troops from Benin, Gabon, Guinea, Nigeria, Senegal, Zaire and Togo. Already disappointed by Oueddei's resistance, and curious to clean up his image before assuming the chairmanship of the OAU, Gaddafi ordered Col Radwan to withdraw all the Libyan troops from Chad in mid-November 1981. Undertaken at the same time, 5,000 US Army troops, two Boeing E-3A Sentry Airborne Early Warning and Control System (AWACS) aircraft, and several Boeing B-52 Stratofortress heavy bombers were deploying to Egypt. This operation was concluded within only three weeks and in a particularly effective fashion. The majority of Libyans and their equipment were evacuated with the help of LAAF transport aircraft, which flew as many as 34 flights from N'Djamena a day in the process. The Libyans even took away all the wreckage of their downed aircraft, destroyed tanks and other vehicles with them, before Radwan led the last column of tanks and jeeps from the Chadian capital towards the Libyan border, almost 1,400 kilometres away. Gaddafi extracted bitter revenge from Chad: Libya closed its bank in N'Djamena and suspended all economic and military aid, causing immense difficulties to the ruined Chadian economy.

The Libyan withdrawal opened the scene for another comeback by Habré. Ignoring the presence of OAU peacekeeping troops, his combatants, led by a number of young officers fresh from training

in France, including Ahmed Gorou, Idris Deby, Hassan Djamous, Ahmed Gorou, and Muhammad Nouri, dashed from bases in Sudan to attack GUNT positions in eastern Chad in May 1982. Equipped with a large number of so-called 'technicals', usually Toyota LandCruiser 4WDs equipped with a wide range of light flak (like ZU-23s, or ZPU-1 and ZPU-4, 14.7mm heavy machine guns), and large numbers of RPG-7s, the FAN force swiftly overpowered several of Oueddei's garrisons.[60] By 7 June 1982, a force of about 2,000 FAN fighters, led by Gorou and Deby, had reached N'Djamena and defeated the GUNT, ending Oueddei's

60 Franziska James, 'Habre's Hour of Glory', *Africa Report*, Sept.–Oct. 1987.

53

reign. Oueddei followed the remnants of his battered military into the mountains of Tibesti massiv, before continuing all the way to Tripoli.

Spoiled Early Call

Despite significant differences with the former Chadian president, the defeat of the GUNT was very bitter for Gaddafi. It resulted in a clearly anti-Libyan government, supported by the USA, France, Egypt and Sudan, establishing itself in a position to 'threaten' the southern border of Libya. It came just a few months after the USA imposed an embargo on imports of Libyan oil (the USA used to buy up to 25% of Libyan oil exports before 1982). Finally, just a day before Habré established himself in power, Israel invaded Lebanon and subsequently caused heavy losses to the armed forces of a major Libyan ally in the Arab world, Syria. Dedicated to avenging this loss of the 'Arab cause', through the rest of 1982 and into 1983, Gaddafi launched several initiatives, including establishing a sort of Libya-sponsored alliance between various international terrorist organisations, inciting unrest and coup attempts in neighbouring countries.

In retaliation for this activity, the Reagan administration began plotting one of the least well-known episodes in the history of aerial warfare related to Libya: 'Operation Early Call'. Run in cooperation with governments and intelligence services of Egypt and Sudan, this involved a phoney, Libyan-sponsored coup against the Sudanese President Numayri, staged in an attempt to entice Gaddafi into sending the LAAF over Khartoum to support the supposed coup-plotters. This would then be engaged in air combats with Egyptian and Sudanese interceptors, supported by US aircraft.

The plan was set in motion during February 1983, with the secret deployment of four USAF E-3A Sentry AWACS aircraft and four McDonnell Douglas KC-10A Extender tankers to Egypt, and the re-deployment of the USS *Nimitz* Carrier Battle Group (CVBG) from a station off Lebanon to a position some 85 miles north of the Egyptian–Libyan border. The US Navy fighters were to protect Egyptian airspace, while E-2Cs and E-3As were planned to vector Egyptian and Sudanese fighters to intercept the Libyans. Although initiated under a thick veil of secrecy, 'Early Call' was effectively thwarted by the US media.

The anti-Numeyri coup attempt, apparently set up by the Sudanese intelligence operatives, was 'foiled'; the *Nimitz* CVBG reached the planned position, and its Tomcats intercepted the first two LAAF MiG-23MS's that appeared in the area on 15 February. However, because of a sand-storm, the USAF E-3As and KC-10s were forced to land at Cairo International instead of Cairo West AB, where they were parked in plain view. Already the following evening, the US media began reporting about this and other related deployments, and Gaddafi, who apparently planned to send the LAAF over Khartoum on Friday 18 February, ordered his air force to stand down. A day later, Reagan ordered the USAF planes to return to their bases, and USS *Nimitz* back to station off Lebanon.[61]

Libya Strikes Back

Although Gaddafi took no action in support of Oueddei during Habré's advance on N'Djamena in mid-1982, Libya welcomed the battered GUNT and Volcan armies, and provided them with sanctuary. Indeed, while keen to show Oueddei that his military could not win a decisive victory in Chad without Libyan support, the Libyan leader could ill-afford to allow a defeat of his Chadian allies. Correspondingly, during late 1982 and early 1983, the GUNT

61 Stanik, pp.74–76.

A T-55 of the 'Islamic Legion', a unit largely consisting of foreigners forcefully recruited by Libya, and deployed in northern Chad for most of the early 1980s. (via Tom Cooper)

and what was left of the Volcan Army were reorganised, re-armed and then re-trained to operate with fire-support from the regular Libyan Army. Lacking patience, Oueddei prematurely rushed a part of his revamped force south from the Aouzou Strip and attacked a garrison at Dourbali held by Habré's forces, in April 1983. In the course of a bitter battle, no less than 142 fighters loyal to the new President of Chad were killed and 252 taken prisoner. Emboldened, Oueddei ordered a continuation of the advance. On 25 June, the GUNT took Faya Largeau and then overran Abéche before starting a march on N'Djamena.

However, by that time the FAN, meanwhile reorganised as the National Armed Forces of Chad (Forces Armées Nationales Tchadiennes, FANT), was alerted and in the process of launching a counteroffensive. Even more so because Habré began receiving help from France, which deployed a team of about 60 operatives of the Foreign Intelligence and Counterespionage Service (Service de Documentation Extérieure et de Contre Espionnage, SDECE) to Chad. These arrived on board a L-100 Hercules transport of the Sfair airline (a company with traditionally close ties to the intelligence circles), in June 1983, together with a load of Milan ATGMs of French origin, and US-made FIM-43A Red Eye MANPADs. Emboldened by this development and together with SDECE operatives, the FANT blocked the GUNT advance and then routed it at Abéche, in early July. Habré's forces then re-took Faya in the course of another bitter battle, fought on 30 and 31 July 1983, and were thus poised to continue their advance into northern Chad. With Oueddei learning the lesson of not engaging without Libyan support, Gaddafi ordered his military into action.

As usual, first on the scene was the LAAF; between 30 July and 2 August 1982, Libyan MiG-23MS's, MiG-23BNs, Mirage F.1s and Su-22s flew at least twenty raids (some including up to sixteen aircraft) on FANT positions in northern Chad, deploying a wide range of conventional bombs (including incendiaries), but also unguided rockets and cannon. This onslaught was further reinforced by Tu-22s forward deployed at Aouzou, and then by tanks and artillery from several Libyan Army battalions grouped into two brigade-sized task forces, which advanced in support of some 3,000 GUNT fighters in the direction of Faya Largeau. The FANT entrenched nearly 5,000 fighters in the Faya area, but these were hopelessly outgunned, despite the presence of the SDECE contingent. The OAU peacekeeping contingent in Chad was supported by three Aermacchi MB.326Ks, four Mirage 5Ms and one SA.330 Puma of the Zairian Air Force (Force Aérienne Zaïroise, FAZA), and a

In August 1982, the LAAF began deploying its most advanced fighter bombers, such as Su-22Ms, one of which can be seen in this photo from August 1981 in Chad. The aircraft was somewhat hampered by its short range, but capable of carrying up to six FAB-500 bombs. Heavier weapons proved more effective when deployed over the soft and sandy soil of Chad, which greatly dampened the effects of lighter bombs. (USN)

One of three FAZA Mirage 5Ms seen on arrival at N'Djamena IAP on 13 July 1982. Despite plenty of opportunities, Zairian Mirages saw no combat in Chad. One of these aircraft (serial M402) was written off under as of yet unknown circumstances. Stripped of all spares, it was dumped in one of corners of N'Djamena IAP. (Albert Grandolini Collection)

This SA.330B Puma of the FAZA was used to haul troops and supplies between various Zairian units deployed in Chad between 1981 and 1983. (Albert Grandolini Collection)

battalion of nearly 1,800 Zairian troops. However, Zairian President Mobutu was unwilling to grant permission for these to become involving in combat. Left on their own, Habré's fighters found themselves attacked by up to 50 LAAF fighter-bombers a day, only sporadically capable of offering any meaningful defence, primarily with help of a few SA-7 MANPADs captured from Libyans during earlier fighting, and French-operated Red Eyes. The MANPADs were used to shoot down two LAAF Su-22/22Ms over Faya, one on 31 July and the other, a leading aircraft from a formation of twelve, on 4 August. However, Libyan firepower subsequently caused the collapse of FANT defences. After all the SDECE operatives were flown out on board one of the ENT's C-47s in the course of two nocturnal sorties, the defences of Faya crumbled on 10 August 1983, with the loss of nearly 700 killed. In a statement provided to the press a few days later, Habré bitterly complained:

Gaddafi is using Soviet tactics, by moving large numbers of planes, tanks and artillery against Faya Largeau. It was genocide … we have seen nothing like this except in films about World War II.[62]

Contrary to Oueddei's spring offensive, the Libyans paused after securing the crucial oasis and the local airfield, intending to first build up a new logistics base before continuing their advance. Contrary to earlier times, this proved to be a crucial mistake: not only was the FANT able to escape to its main base in N'Djamena, but also two major superpowers were now about to react to the renewed Libyan intervention.

Operation Manta
Even with hindsight, it might appear that the US reaction to the new Libyan intervention in Chad remained limited. The US Navy deployed the CVBG centred on the carrier USS *Eisenhower* (*CVN-69*) off Libya's coast. On 1 August 1983, F-14s from VF-143 chased away two LAAF MiG-23s that approached for inspection, prompting Gaddafi to threaten his military would sink the carrier if it entered the Gulf of Syrte. However, except for deploying two E-3As, two KC-10As and eight F-15s supported by 600 ground personnel to

62 'France intervenes in Chad Civil War', *Time*, 16 Aug. 1983.

Sudan on 7 August 1983, seemingly Washington appeared not ready to get involved with Libya again.

Actually, the Reagan administration pursued a strategy of psychological warfare directed at France as much as at Libya, with the aim of pressuring a reluctant government in Paris to assume primary responsibility for the defence of its former colony. As soon as the new Libyan invasion started, the USA offered US$10 million in military aid to Habré's government (subsequently upped to US$25 million), and a handful of US military advisors deployed to train FANT troops how to use FIM-43A Redeye MANPADs. The USA then arranged an airlift of 700 additional Zairian troops to secure N'Djamena. All of this confronted President Francois Mitterrand of France with an implicit challenge: if the French failed to aid Habré, they would not only be shown up as less willing than the USA, but also unable to show strength to Gaddafi. This in turn would have negative consequences for their influence in a number of African states governed by 'moderate' administrations, many of which were already under Libyan pressure.

Contrary to Mitterrand, the French military was keen to launch an intervention and already developing contingency plans, one of which envisaged 'Operation Orque': an attack on Aouzou airfield by six Jaguars based at M'Poko IAP, outside Bangui in the CAR, followed by a drop of an entire parachute regiment on Faya Largeau. Obviously this idea was risky, not only because of the huge distance (nearly 2,050 kilometres) the single-seat fighter-bombers would have to cross in order to reach their target, but also because such an operation would require support from vulnerable C-135F tankers and C.160 Transall transports, which in turn would expose

In August 1983, the USN deployed the second ship of the Nimitz-class, USS *Eisenhower* (*CVN-69*), off the Libyan coast. This photograph shows that carrier accompanied by the guided missile cruiser USS *Belknap* (*CG-26*) and three Egyptian missile boats. (USN)

Column of Foreign Legion troops, mounted on VLRA trucks, two of which have been modified as 'technicals', equipped with 20mm cannons. This truck proved highly popular in Chad, not only for its reliability, but also because of its long range of nearly 1,000 kilometres. (Albert Grandolini Collection)

themselves to interception by LAAF jets. Furthermore, Orque was not promising to deliver the desired effect and stave off the Libyans and the GUNT. Instead, on 5 August 1983, Mitterand ordered the military to launch a large-scale intervention in Chad: 'Operation Manta'.

The deployment of the French military into Chad began almost immediately, with one company of the 8th RPIMa transferring from Cameroon to N'Djamena International on 11 August 1983. Once this crucial installation was secured, AdA Transalls began deploying

a contingent of 1,500 troops of the Foreign Legion, supported by armoured cars and light artillery. These were followed by an ALAT detachment of five Aérospatiale SA.342 Gazelle helicopters of the 1st and 2nd Combat Helicopter Regiments (Régiment d'Hélicoptères de Combat, RHC), armed with HOT anti-tank guided missiles (ATGMs), and three Cessna L-19 light aircraft. While some of the ground troops subsequently deployed along the road from the Chadian capital in the direction of Abéche, aerial operations were hampered by the debilitating state of N'Djamena IAP. This was found not only to have been neglected for years but also largely destroyed by several battles, and the French had to rebuild it practically from scratch. While the construction work was going on, there was no kerosene at N'Djamena IAP nor place for operations of larger aircraft. The fuel had to be hauled in with the help of C-135Fs and DC-8s of the Minerve airlines to M'Poko, where it was re-loaded to much smaller Transalls for transportation to Chad. M'Poko IAP eventually turned into the centrepiece of the entire operation, then Boeing 747s of Air France and UTA, which were used to haul most of the troops and equipment for Operation Manta, could not land at N'Djamena. Therefore, their cargo had also to be re-loaded to C.160s at M'Poko. Considering that a single B747 could carry as much as ten Transalls, it is unsurprising that the AdA ended operating no less than 26 C.160s between Chad and the CAR. Similarly, the AdA's contingent that was to support Manta which initially included four Jaguars, four Mirage F.1Cs, and one C-135F, remained on alert at M'Poko for the time being.

Meanwhile, the ALAT did manage to deploy several SA.330B Puma helicopters from the 5th RHC ALAT to N'Djamena, while the AdA established an AAA site supported by a SNERI mobile

An AML-90 armoured car of the Foreign Legion seen accompanied by an ALAT Gazelle, armed with a HOT ATGM (small tube on the side of the helicopter). High temperatures and dusty conditions caused lots of problems with maintenance of Gazelles, and limited them to carry only two HOT ATGMs, instead of the more usual four. (Albert Grandolini Collection)

An AdA SNERI mobile radar station as seen in the field in Chad in August 1983. By the end of that year, the French operated four such radar stations in the country. (Albert Grandolini Collection)

A DC-8 transport of the AdA, seen while unloading equipment for Operation Manta at N'Djamena IAP. (Albert Grandolini Collection)

Gunners of an AdA flak battery protecting N'Djamena IAP monitoring a Jaguar A of EC.11 rolling by in late August 1983. (Albert Grandolini Collection)

early warning radar. During the following weeks, two additional mobile radar sets of the same type were positioned in Moussoro and Ati, while the ALAT operated a fourth radar station with a similar system in Biltine. Once most of the work at N'Djamena IAP was completed, the AdA contingent moved in on 21 August 1983. By then it included six Jaguar As of EC.3/11 'Corse', four Mirage F.1Cs of EC.1/5 'Vendée', two C-135Fs of ERV.93, and two Atlantics of 22F.

With the French government not keen to become fully involved in a new war, the plan for Manta was actually quite limited. Its aim was to secure Habré's government through the deployment of French forces in N'Djamena and Abéche, followed by the establishment of the so-called 'Red Line' along the 15th Parallel, a blocking position, the purpose of which was to stop any advance of Gaddafi's or Oueddei's troops into southern Chad. Despite its limitations, Manta proved effective. Not keen to fight France, the Libyans discontinued their advance and the situation 'froze' for the next few months.

Skirmishes along the Red Line
During the summer of 1983, the Libyans largely respected the French presence, and LAAF fighters never crossed the 'Red Line', although they continued flying air strikes against various of FANT-

held positions and to the north. In early September 1983, when the FANT and the GUNT clashed several times in the Oum Chalouba area, the French felt prompted to 'send another message', and two Jaguars flew several simulated strafing runs over GUNT positions, causing a panic and a rather hurried withdrawal in a northerly direction. Although French military intelligence estimated that the LAAF was operating no less than 92 combat aircraft inside Chad in October and November 1983 (including 40 planes based at Aouzou), of which 22 were Mirage F.1s, ten Mirage 5s, 27 Su-22/22Ms, six Tu-22s, and no less than 27 SF.260s, none of these appeared to interrupt AdA operations. Ali Tani recalled:

We received strict orders not to fly south of the Red Line. We flew patrols along it on the northern side, and the French due south. The closest I came to engaging the French was on 2 September, when I detected one or two Jaguars in Oum Chalouba area. They never came within the range of my weapons. A colleague of mine flew Mirage F.1EDs and he encountered one French Mirage F.1C, later the same month, but nobody fired.[63]

Although no French accounts about such 'chance meetings' with LAAF fighters are known, two AdA Mirages did intercept a lone

63 Note that French sources indicate the later encounter described here should have occurred during the 'Operation Épervier', in 1986, which is to be described in Part 2 of this book.

Operation Manta saw the first deployment of the Mirage F.1C-200 interceptors to Chad. These two F.1Cs from EC.5 can be seen in front of one of FAZA's Mirages and two MB.326Ks, at N'Djamena IAP. (Albert Grandolini Collection)

Due to a shortage of tankers, French combat aircraft often depended on C.160 Transall Licornes for in-flight refuelling. (Albert Grandolini Collection)

Early during Operation Manta, the French experienced significant problems with the supply of kerosene for AdA's combat aircraft deployed to Chad. This photograph shows a Jaguar being refuelled directly from a C.160 Transall Licorne, on the tarmac of N'Djamena IAP. (Albert Grandolini Collection)

By February 1984, when this photograph of two EC.11's Jaguars equipped with Barracuda ECM-pods was taken, the AdA contingent supporting Manta operated no less than eight Jaguars, seven Mirage F.1Cs, two C-135Fs, two Atlantics and up to 30 transport aircraft from N'Djamena IAP. (Albert Grandolini Collection)

LAAF Il-76 that was flying north of Salal on 23 October 1983. As soon as the French warned the Libyan crew to distance themselves, the transport immediately turned in a northerly direction.

Incidents of a different kind have left a very bitter taste between AdA pilots deployed in Chad. On 25 January 1984, a column of about 25 GUNT vehicles, including several fuel and water tankers, as well as technicals equipped with ZU-23 flaks, crossed the Red Line and attacked the FANT post in Ziguey, near the border to Niger. About a dozen of the FANT troops were massacred and the insurgents then kidnapped two Belgian citizens that worked for Doctors Without Borders (Médicins Sans Frontières, MSF). As the GUNT column began its withdrawal towards the north, it was detected by a Jaguar and a Mirage F.1C, at around 11:00am local time. However, the pilots were not authorised to attack; instead they could only report what they saw to their HQ in N'Djamena, while this was in turn conferring with Paris. Three hours later, three Jaguars returned to find the column in the Torodoum area, and at around 4:00pm it was detected again, still in the same area, though this time by two Jaguar As and a Mirage F.1C. While attempting to establish the exact composition and strength of the GUNT force, the French fighter-bombers came under ground fire and their pilots requested permission to return fire, prompting another

radio-conference between N'Djamena and Paris.[64] Independently from this short engagement the crew of an ALAT Gazelle found an insurgent Toyota technical that was left behind and destroyed it with a single HOT ATGM.

Military commanders in N'Djamena were still discussing their options and waiting for orders from reluctant politicians in Paris about one hour later, when the next AdA patrol – consisting of two Jaguars from EC.4/11 'Jura' escorted by a Mirage F.1C – came under fire from ZU-23 flaks. Namely, almost 800 kilometres away from their base, the pilots found it extremely difficult not only to find the GUNT column (meanwhile hidden underneath palm trees) but especially to identify what vehicles were dangerous and which were carrying the hijacked MSF workers. In a courageous, but nearly suicidal attempt to take a closer look, Captain Croci descended to make a low altitude pass, but his Jaguar received a hit in the hydraulic system. The pilot attempted to eject from minimal altitude but was killed in the process. The remaining Jaguar and the Mirage then attacked the column and destroyed several technicals with gunfire, before the F.1C was hit by ground fire as well. Supported by one C-135F tanker, the damaged Mirage returned safely to N'Djamena IAP.

---

64 As of 1984, the French military did not operate satellite communications. This proved to be one of the major problems during Operation Manta, because it took a very long time to transmit situation reports to Paris and receive a reply.

The crew of this SA.342 Gazelle was photographed while re-loading ammunition for a 20mm cannon that was positioned to fire out of the left-hand doors of the helicopter. (Albert Grandolini Collection)

While officially declaring the loss of its fighter-bomber as occurring during a 'reconnaissance mission', the government in Paris was angered enough to order three battalions of the Foreign Legion to be deployed along the Red Line, in order to prevent any similar incursions in the future.

Due to the unpopularity of Operation Manta with the French public, the government in Paris was concerned to keep this intervention in Chad as a 'low profile affair'. Correspondingly, a number of skirmishes that occurred in Chad during late 1983 and early 1984 remain unrecorded and very little is known about what was going on. Considering that the AdA's involvement in Operation Manta was at its peak in February 1984, when no less than eight Jaguars, seven Mirage F.1Cs, two KC-135s, two Atlantics, three DC-8 transports and up to 26 C.160 Transalls were deployed in the country (in addition to about 30 Gazelles and Pumas of the ALAT!), it is certain that there were additional reasons for concern. However, the only 'hard' piece of information that ever emerged was related to the loss of another Jaguar on 16 may 1984. This time an aircraft from EC.3/11, flown by Cdte Bernard Voelckel, hit a sand dune during a low-altitude mission in the Oum Chalouba area, and crashed some fifteen kilometres from the Siltou dam, killing the pilot.

Phony Withdrawal

Supposedly concerned about dissent between the GUNT and Libyan Army forces in April 1984, Gaddafi offered a 'unilateral' withdrawal of his troops from Chad. More than happy to accept such an offer, Paris entered negotiations with Tripoli. Following several months of talks, on 17 September 1984 both parties announced their intention to withdraw. Actually, this was Gaddafi's ploy; while the French began pulling their troops out, with the last of these having left the country by 11 November 1984 (most of AdA's Jaguars were re-deployed to M'Poko IAP, meanwhile), the Libyans scattered their forces and camouflaged them in the deserts of northern Chad. Simultaneously, they intensified their work on expanding airfields in Aouzou and Faya Largeau, and started work on the construction of a major new base near the Wadi Doum dam, some 200 kilometres north-east of Faya.[65]

The withdrawal of French forces from Chad was undertaken within the framework of 'Operation Mirmillon'. In order to distract the Libyans away from southern Chad, the French Navy deployed its carrier *Foch (R-99)* off the Libyan coast. Obviously, the LAAF could not ignore the appearance of Aéronavale's aircraft along its border and on 15 October 1984 it scrambled two Mirage 5s to intercept the F-8E(FN) Crusader flown by Lt Cdr Serge Hébert. After a short engagement in the course of which Hébert skilfully outmanoeuvred both opponents, the Libyans withdrew from the scene quite quickly.[66]

Subsequently, AdA's Mirage IV reconnaissance bombers were

---

65 The construction of the runway at Wadi Doum was quite simple, and adapted to local circumstances. Faced with the problem of having to harden the soft sand soil, the Libyans poured tons of oil over it, and then used metal plates imported from East Germany to construct a 3,800 metres long runway.

66 Collectif, *Chronique du Charles de Gaulle; L'apogée d'un siècle d'aéronautique navale*, p. 121.

Tensions caused by Libyan intervention in Chad reached a point where France imposed an arms embargo upon Libya in August 1983. Correspondingly, five LAAF Mirage 5Ds (serials 428, 429, 433, 438, and 439), and two Mirage 5DRs (serials 304 and 360) were impounded at the Dassault plant in Toulouse-Colomiers. It seems that none of the aircraft in question was returned to Libya, and all were taken by the AdA. (Fana de l'Aviation Archives)

deployed to fly reconnaissance sorties over northern Chad, designed to track down Libyan dispositions in northern Chad and follow the construction works in Wadi Doum. In the course of 'Operation Ombrine', the Mirage IVA (serial number 9, coded AH) flown by Cdte Arzul and Capt Duffaut thundered high above Wadi Doum on 18 November 1984. Only six days later, the same plane was flown by Lt Col Sabathe and Cdte Mérouze for a 10 hour mission code-named 'Operation Martre', that covered Gouro, Fada, Wadi Doum and Faya Largeau. Amongst others, these missions established that the number of LAAF aircraft deployed at Aouzou airfield decreased to only nine Su-22/22Ms and nine Mirage F.1s.[67]

By the end of 1984, and through early 1985, additional reconnaissance missions, including Operations codenamed 'Brama', 'Retine', 'Tégénaire' and 'Musaraigne', were flown by tactical reconnaissance fighters over Wadi Doum, Faya Largeau and Fada. The LAAF did not manage to intercept any of these sorties, although it operated a well-equipped radar network in this area, including a concentration of one SA-6 and one SA-13 SAM-site, supported by two batteries of ZSU-23-4 SPAAGs at Wadi Doum. Further details have become available only about Operations Musaraigne III and IV, flown by AdA Jaguars based at M'Poko IAP, outside Bangui. The first of these was undertaken by Cdte Chanel and Lt Didier from EC.3/3 'Ardennes' on 7 December 1985. Each aircraft was equipped with RP.36 underwing drop tanks with a capacity of 1,200 litres, a RP.36P container with reconnaissance cameras under the fuselage, a Phimat chaff and flare dispenser under the left outboard underwing pylon and a Barracuda jammer pod under the right outboard underwing pylon. Launched at 7:30am from M'Poko IAP, Musaraigne III lasted four hours and included one in-flight refuelling operation from a C-135F on the way to target (during which one of the Jaguars involved collided with the refuelling basket, resulting in a damaged Barracuda pod), and one on the way back to the base.

Operation Musaraigne IV was launched around 12:30pm local time on the same day from M'Poko IAP, and included Jaguars flown

67 Air Fan No. 25.

A Puma-Pirate. In the best traditions of Chadian deployments, this ALAT SA.330B was modified to carry a 20mm cannon that was positioned to fire through the right cabin doors. (Albert Grandolini Collection)

by Captains Antoine (on A82) and Vinson (though with two 'spares' taking off as well, in case of any technical malfunctions). After taking fuel from a C-135F some 300 kilometres north of Bangui, the two French fighters proceeded at an altitude of 15,000ft (4,572m) to make a photo-reconnaissance run along the line connecting Chicha and Yogoun. These two Jaguars returned to M'Poko at 4:15pm local time, after another IFR-operation from a C-135F was waiting for them south of the Red Line. The films from these two missions were developed in situ and then transferred to the Centre d'Interprétation Photographique de l'Armée de l'Air (CIPAA), later the same evening. Ironically, it was only on the basis of newspaper reports on the next day, that the involved pilots learned that they were tracked by a Libyan SA-6 SAM-site during the mission. One of the results of these two sorties was the conclusion that Wadi Doum AB was not only operational, but with a 3,800 metre long runway capable of supporting the heaviest aircraft in the Libyan arsenal,

Table 3: Confirmed Attrition of AdA, Aéronavale, ALAT, ENT & LAAF Aircraft in Chad, 1978–1985

Date	Unit	Aircraft	Serial or Registration & Construction Number	Notes
2nd February 1969	AdA EAA.1/21	AD-4N	49	hit the sea off Gabon; Lt Decambre KIA
14th June 1969	AdA ELAA.1/22	AD-4N	43	crashed at Fort Lamy; Capt Bertand OK
1st October 1969	AdA ELAA.1/22	AD-4N	59	crashed at Fort Lamy; Lt Pastorelli OK
26th August 1970	AdA ELAA.1/22	AD-4N	26	belly landing at Fort Lamy; pilot OK
3rd September 1970	AdA ELAA.1/22	AD-4N	79	engine failure near Fada; Lt Barando OK
8th September 1970	AdA ELAA.1/22	AD-4N	85	emergency landing at Zouar; pilot OK
18th February 1971	ALAT?	PA.22	unknown	crashed or shot down near Am Dagachi; WO Dartigaux, Maj Puloch, Lt Laval-Gilly KIA
21st February 1971	AN 33F	HSS-1	454	crashed in Bardai; crew OK
29th January 1978	ENT	C-47	TT-LAE/77049	shot down by FROLINAT SA-7 in Borkou area; pilot Gilbert Legoff and crew killed
30th January 1978	ENT	C-54	TT-NAA/42936	shot down by FROLINAT SA-7 in Faya Largeau area; crew of five injured but recovered safely
16th April 1978	ENT	AD-4N	unknown	shot down by FROLINAT SA-7 in Salal area; French pilot Sgt Jean-Louis Latour KIA
31st May 1978	AdA EC.3/11	Jaguar A	A52/???	shot down by FROLINAT DShK machine gun in Djedda area; Lt Col Léon Pachebat ejected safely
8th August 1978	AdA EC.2/11	Jaguar A	A109/???	crashed north of Djedda; Lt Robert Jacquel (EC.1/11) KIA
23rd August 1978	AdA EC.2/11	Jaguar A	A111/???	collided with Jaguar A97; Lt J Francois (EC.1/11) ejected safely
14th October 1978	AdA EC.1/11	Jaguar A	A106/???	crashed on landing at N'Djamena IAP; Capt Serge Lineman (EC.1/7) KIA
8th or 9th December 1980	LAAF No. 1325 Sqn	Mi-25	103	shot down by FAN ground fire in N'Djamena; crew, including Col Abdul Khalifa Mohammed Amer, was KIA
16th September 1981	LAAF No. 1160 Sqn	SF.260WL	341	shot down by ground fire; crew of two KIA
31st July 1983	LAAF No.1032 Sqn	Su-22M or Su-22M-3K	unknown	shot down by FAN SA-7 over Faya Largeau; Maj Abdul Salam Sharaf ad-Din PoW
4th August 1983	LAAF No. 1032 Sqn	Su-22M or Su-22M-3K	unknown	shot down by FAN SA-7 over Faya Largeau; pilot recovered
25th January 1984	AdA EC.2/11	Jaguar A	A81/11-MA	shot down by GUNT ZU-23 in Torodoum area; Capt Michel Croci (EC.4/11) KIA
16th April 1984	AdA EC.4/11	Jaguar A	A125/11-YM	crashed 14km from Siltou, Oum Chalouba area; Cdte Bernard Voelckel (EC.3/11) KIA

including Tu-22 bombers and Il-76 transports. Of course, this realisation led to calls for an attack on the site and the destruction of the runway. Correspondingly, planning was started in December 1985, and even resulted in a training sortie involving six Jaguars (led by Capt Antoine on aircraft with serial A153) and four Mirage F.1Cs flown from M'Poko against a simulated target in Awakaba on 19th of the same month. However, for unknown reasons, Paris first delayed, and eventually cancelled this operation.

Tensions in Chad thus appeared to be lessening during mid-1985. However, as subsequent developments were to show, this was only the 'calm before the storm'. Much more action, including a period of some of the most intensive air warfare ever to occur over Libya was to follow within a few months.

Bibliography

Much of the material presented in this book was obtained in the course of research for the book series 'Arab MiGs', which presents the history of Arab air forces at war with Israel. Additional information was acquired during interviews with participants and eyewitnesses mentioned in the acknowledgments and elsewhere: in Egypt and Libya, but also in France, USA, Iraq and Syria. Sadly, earlier very serious and very direct threats to the security of specific persons prevented most of them from speaking openly, while availability of original Libyan documentation remains very limited. Nevertheless, the contributions of all persons that provided their recollections proved precious and greatly assisted the authors in the preparation and publication of this book:

Beaumont, H., *Mirage III, Mirage 5, Mirage 50: Toutes les versions en France et dans le Monde* (Clichy Cedex, Larivière, 2005, ISBN 2-84890-079-2)

Bévillard, Gen A., *La Saga du Transport Aérien Militaire Francais, De Kolwezi à Mazar-e-Sharif, de Port au Prence à Dumont-d'Urville, Tome 1* (Sceaux, l'Esprit du Livre Editions, 2007)

Blundy, D., & Lycett, A., *Qaddafi and the Libyan Revolution* (Boston, Little Brown & Co, 1987, ISBN 978-0-316-10042-7)

Brent, W., *African Air Forces* (Freeworld Publications, 1999)

Bugakov, I. S., Ivanov, B. V., Kartashev, V. B., Laverntev, A. P., Ligav, V. A. & Pashoko, V. A., *Kazan Helicopters: Flight Goes On* (Vertolet Publisher and Kazan Helicopters, 2001)

Buijtenhuijs, R., *Le Frolinat et les guerres civiles du Tchad, 1977-1984* (Paris, Karthala, 1987)

Cadiou, Y., *Opération Limousin au Tchad de 1969 à 1972* (anciens-combattants.forumactif.com)

Cadiou, Y., *Opex Tacaud* (operationtacaud.wordpress.com)

Chambost, G., *Missions de guerre: Histoires authentiques* (Altipresse, 2003, ISBN 978-2911218255)

Chenel, B., Liebert, M., & Moreau, E., *Mirage III/5/50 en service à l'étranger* (Le Vigen, LELA Presse, 2014)

Cochrane, J. & Elliott, S., *Military Aircraft Insignia of the World* (Shrewsbury, Airlife Publishing, 1998, ISBN 1-85310-873-1)

Collectif, *Chronique du Charles de Gaulle; L'apogée d'un siècle d'aéronautique navale* (Chroniques Them, N.D., ISBN 978-2205053-23-4)

Cooper, T., Nicolle, D., with Nordeen, L., Salti, P., and Smisek, M., *Arab MiGs Volume 4: Attrition War, 1967–1973* (Houston, Harpia Publishing, 2013, ISBN 978-0-9854554-1-5)

Cooper, T., 'Darfur – Krieg der Antonow Bomber', *Fliegerrevue Extra* magazine (Germany), Vol. 20/March 2008

Cooper, T., 'Geheime Helfer im Yom-Kippour Krieg', *Fliegerrevue Extra* magazine (Germany), Vol. 13/June 2006

Cooper, T., 'Tschad: Hintergründe', script for briefing on situation in Chad, delivered to the Offiziersgesellschaft Wien, 3 April 2008 (Austria)

Cooper, T., '45 Years of Wars and Insurgencies in Chad', *Truppendienst* magazine (Austria), Vol. 6/2009

Cooper, T., Weinert P., Hinz F. & Lepko M., *African MiGs, MiGs and Sukhois in Service in Sub-Saharan Africa, Volume 1: Angola to Ivory Coast* (Vienna, Harpia Publishing, 2010, ISBN 978-0-9825539-5-4)

Cooper, T., Weinert P., Hinz F. & Lepko M., *African MiGs, MiGs and Sukhois in Service in Sub-Saharan Africa, Volume 2: Madagascar to Zimbabwe* (Vienna, Harpia Publishing, 2011, ISBN 978-0-9825539-8-5)

Dupuy, T. N. (Col, US Army, ret.), and Blanchard W. (Col, US Army, ret.) *The Almanac of World Military Power* (Dunn Loring/London, T. N. Dupuy Associates/Arthur Barker Ltd., 1972, ISBN 0-213-16418-3)

Flintham, V., *Air Wars and Aircraft: a Detailed Record of Air Combat 1945 to the Present* (London, Arms and Armour Press, 1989, ISBN 0-85368-779-X)

Forget, Gen M., *Nos forces aériennes en Opex, Un demi-siècle d'intervention extérieures* (Paris, Economica, 2013)

Glassman, J. D., *Arms for the Arabs: The Soviet Union and the War in the Middle East* (Baltimore, The John Hopkins University Press, 1975, ISBN 0-8018-1747-1)

Gomez, E., *Le Tchad vu par un aviateur* (fncv.com)

Guillemin, S., *Les Skyraiders français* (Outreau, Lela Presse, 2012)

Heikal, H. M., *The 30 Years War* (in Arabic), (Cairo, el-Ahram Publishing & Translation Centre, 1990, Reg. No. 5063/1990)

Huertas, S. M., *Dassault-Breguet Mirage III/5* (London, Osprey Publishing, 1990, ISBN 0-85045-933-8)

Kotlobovskiy, A. B., *MiG-21 in Local Wars* (in Russian), (Kiev, ArchivPress, 1997)

Koszela, B. Bedo-Tchad, *Le combat de Bedo au Tchad (BET) le 11 october 1970* (aha-helico-air.asso.fr)

Liébert, M. & Buyck, S., *Le Mirage F1 et les Mirage de seconde generation à voilure en fleche, Vol. 1: Projets et Prototypes* (Outreau, Éditions Lela Presse, ISBN 2-914017-40-5)

Liébert, M. & Buyck, S., *Le Mirage F1 et les Mirage de seconde generation à voilure en fleche, Vol.2: Les Mirage F1 desérie, Un avion aux multiples facettes* (Outreau, Éditions Lela Presse, ISBN 2-914017-41-3)

Menahim, Maj Gen A. K. al-, *Egyptian Wars in Modern History* (in Arabic), (Beirut, Dar Mustakbal al-Arabi, 1990)

Neau, J., *L'intervention de la France dans le conflit tchadien, 1969-1975: Une guerre révolutionnaire introuvable, un fiasco en position de force* (Mémoires d'hommes, 2006, ISBN 978-2843670237)

Nicolle, D., & Cooper, T., *Arab MiG-19 and MiG-21 Units in Combat* (Oxford, Osprey Publishing Ltd., 2004, ISBN 1-84176-655-0)

Nordeen, L, & Nicolle D., *Phoenix over the Nile* (Washington, Smithsonian, 1996, ISBN 1-56098-826-3)

Okasha, Maj Gen M., *Soldiers in the Sky* (in Arabic), (Cairo, Ministry of Defence, 1976)

Pollack, Kenneth M., *Arabs at War: Military Effectiveness, 1948–1991* (Univesity of Nebraska Press, 2004, ISBN 0-8032-8783-6)

Sadat, A. el-, *In Search of Identity* (Harper & Row Publishers Inc., 1977)

Sené, F., *Raids Dans le Sahara Central Tchad Lybie 1941–1987: Sarra Ou le Rezzou Decisif* (L'Harmattan, 2011, ISBN 978-2296566446)

Shazly, S. el-, *The Crossing of the Suez* (San Francisco, American Mideast Research, 2003, ISBN 0-9604562-2-8)

Spartacus, Col., *Opération Manta: Tchad 1983–1984* (Omnibus, 1985, ISBN 978-2259013307)

Stafrace, C., *Arab Air Forces* (Carolton, Squadron/Signal Publications Inc., 1994, ISBN 0-89747-326-4)

Stafrace, C., *The Air Campaign for the Freedom of Libya, February to October 2011, Operations Odyssey Dawn and Unified Protector* (Camouflage & Markings Number 6), (Bletchley, Guideline Publications, 2012)

Stanik, Joseph T., *El Dorado Canyon: Reagan's Undeclared War with Qaddafi* (Annapolis, Naval Institute Press, ISBN 1-55750-983-2)

Tanks of the World: Taschenbuch der Panzer (Koblenz, Bernard & Graefe Verlag, 1990, ISBN 3-7637-5871-2)

Thompson, Sir R. (editor), *War in Peace: An Analysis of Warfare since 1945* (London, Orbis Publishing, 1981, ISBN 0-85613-341-8)

Tonquédec, Pierre de, *Face à Kadhafi – Opération Tacaud Tchad, 1978–1980* (SOTECA, 2012, ISBN 978-2916385907)

Turner, J. W., *Continent Ablaze: The Insurgency Wars in Africa 1960 to the Present* (London, Arms & Armour Press, 1998, ISBN 1-85409-128-X)

Vezin, Alain, *Jaguar, le félin en action* (Boulogne, ETAI, 2008)

Willis D. (editor), *Aerospace Encyclopaedia of World Air Forces* (London, Aerospace Publishing Ltd., 1999, ISBN 1-86184-045-4)

Zaloga, Steven J., *Red SAM: The SA-2 Guideline Anti-Aircraft Missile* (Oxford: Osprey Publishing Ltd, 2007) ISBN 978-1-84603-062-8

Zolotaryov, Maj Gen V. A., *Russia in Local Wars and Military Conflicts in the Second Half of the 20th Century* (in Russian), (Moscow, Institute of Military History, Ministry of Defence of the Russian Federation, 2000)

World Defence Almanac, *Military Technology* magazine volumes 1/91, 1/93, 1/95, 1/97, 1/98 & 1/03

Various volumes of *El-Djeich* magazine (the official publication of the Algerian Ministry of Defence), *Air Fan, le Fana de l'Aviation, Aviation Magazine Internationale, Air et Cosmos,* and *Raids* (France), *Aviation News* magazine (UK), and personal notes of all the authors based on other various daily and weekly printed publications.

Acknowledgments

The authors wish to express their special gratitude to all those individuals who contributed to this book. Foremost are several former Libyan Air Force pilots that were forced to leave their country at the time because of issues related to their own, and the safety of their families. Some of them have granted interviews only on condition of anonymity, and thus we would like to pass on our special thanks for providing advice, unique information and insights to Abdoul Hassan, Ali Tani and Hazem al-Bajigni.

Several retired US Navy pilots and officers have kindly provided advice and interviews too, although, again because of clear, direct and very specific threats for their personal security, they also felt forced to do so on condition of anonymity. The few exceptions we feel free to mention include Lawrence 'Music' Muczynski and Dave 'Hey Joe' Parsons, to whom we wish to express our special thanks.

We would also like to thank several retired French Air Force pilots, servicemen and members of their families, who kindly provided permission to use their documentation, family archives and photographs. Sadly, with the exception of Bernard Lart and Jean-Marie Lipka, we do not feel at liberty to publicly name anybody else, and will only be able to forward our thanks privately.

Further thanks go to a number of researchers elsewhere, who kindly helped during the work on this book. In particular, Group 73 and friends in Egypt, Brigadier-General Ahmad Sadik from Iraq, Dr. David Nicolle and Mike Bennett in Great Britain, Tom Long in the USA, Arthur Hubers and Jeroen Nijemeijer from the Netherlands, Robert Szombati from Hungary, and Pit Weinert from Germany. All of them, in one form or another, provided extensive aid and related research to make this book possible.

Tom Cooper

Tom Cooper, from Austria, is a military-aviation journalist and historian. Following a career in a worldwide transportation business – in which, during his extensive travels in Europe and the Middle East, he established excellent contacts – he moved into writing. An earlier fascination with post-Second World War military aviation has narrowed to focus on smaller air forces and conflicts, about which he has collected extensive archives of material. Concentrating primarily on air warfare that has previously received scant attention, he specializes in investigative research on little-known African and Arab air forces, as well as the Iranian Air Force. Cooper has published 21 books – including the unique 'Arab MiGs' series, which examines the deployment and service history of major Arab air forces in conflicts with Israel – as well as over 200 articles on related topics, providing a window into a number of previously unexamined yet fascinating conflicts and relevant developments.

Albert Grandolini

Military historian and aviation-journalist, Albert Grandolini, was born in France and gained an MA in history from Paris I Sorbonne University. His primary research focus is on contemporary conflicts in general and particularly on the military history of Asia. Having spent his childhood in South Vietnam, the Vietnam War has been one of his main fields of research. He is the author of the books *Fall of the Flying Dragon: South Vietnamese Air Force (1973–1975)* with Harpia Publishing and *Armor of the Vietnam War: Asian Forces*, Concord Publishing, and is also co-author of the three volumes of the Libyan Air Wars with Helion Publishers in the Africa@War Series. He has also written numerous articles for various British, French and German magazines, such as *Air Enthusiast, Flieger Revue Extra, Fana de l'aviation, Tank Zone* and *Batailles et Blindés*. He has regularly contributed to the Air Combat Information Group (ACIG) and the Au Delà de la Colline military history French website.

Arnaud Delalande

Arnaud Delalande is researcher and author from Tours in France. Military history, and the history of military aviation in particular have long been his passion, especially airpower in Africa and in former French colonies. Except for working as editor of 'Aéro Histo' blog (http://aerohisto.blogspot.fr) and contributor of 'Alliance Geostrategique' blog (alliancegeostrategique.org) in his spare time, he has become one of few foreigners with deeper interest in the history of recent Chadian wars, as well as French military operations in that country. He has published several related articles in specialized French magazines such as *Air Fan*, and *Air Combat*. He is also co-author of the three volumes of the Libyan Air Wars with Helion Publishers in the Africa@War Series.